knit or crochet

Have It Your Way

knit *or* crochet

Have It Your Way

15 Fun Projects
with Complete Hook and
Needle Instructions for Each

Creative Publishing
international

**Creative Publishing
international**

First published in the United States of America by
Creative Publishing international, Inc., a member of
Quayside Publishing Group
400 First Avenue North
Suite 300
Minneapolis, MN 55401
1-800-328-3895
www.creativepub.com

ISBN-13: 978-1-58923-431-4
ISBN-10: 1-58923-431-6

10 9 8 7 6 5 4 3 2 1

Library of Congress Cataloging-in-Publication Data
Hubert, Margaret.
  Knit or crochet - have it your way / Margaret Hubert.
    p. cm.
  ISBN-13: 978-1-58923-431-4
  ISBN-10: 1-58923-431-6
  1. Knitting--Patterns. 2. Crocheting--Patterns. I. Title.
  TT820.H833 2009
  746.43'2041--dc22

                                        2008031272

Technical Editors: Rita Greenfeder and Karen Manthey
Copy Editor: India Tresselt
Proofreader: Lucia Raatma
Cover and Book Design: Rachel Fitzgibbon
Page Layout: Rachel Fitzgibbon
Photography: Ned Witrogen

Printed in China

contents

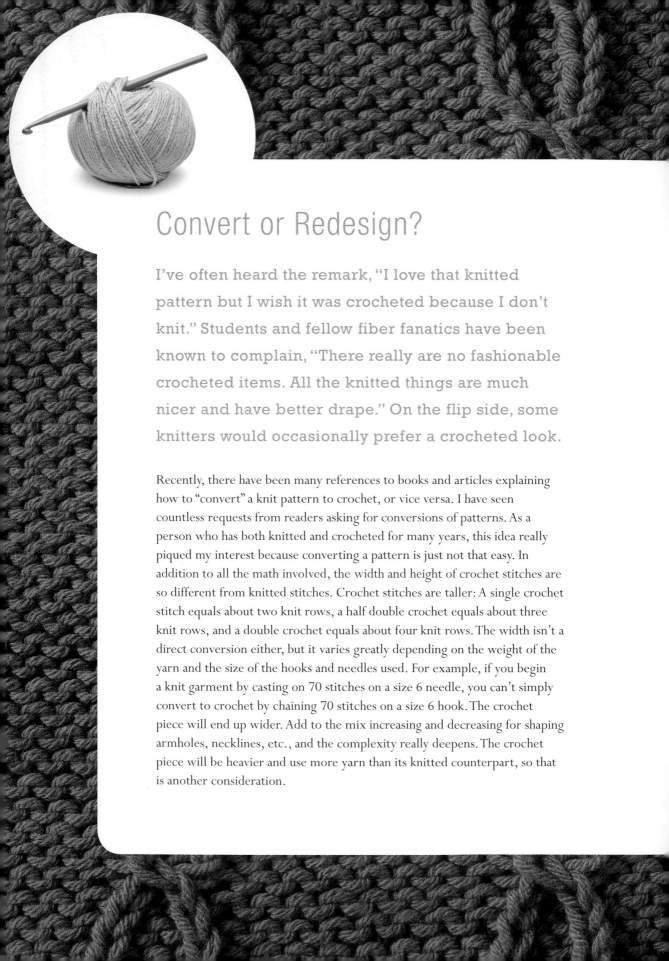

Convert or Redesign?

I've often heard the remark, "I love that knitted pattern but I wish it was crocheted because I don't knit." Students and fellow fiber fanatics have been known to complain, "There really are no fashionable crocheted items. All the knitted things are much nicer and have better drape." On the flip side, some knitters would occasionally prefer a crocheted look.

Recently, there have been many references to books and articles explaining how to "convert" a knit pattern to crochet, or vice versa. I have seen countless requests from readers asking for conversions of patterns. As a person who has both knitted and crocheted for many years, this idea really piqued my interest because converting a pattern is just not that easy. In addition to all the math involved, the width and height of crochet stitches are so different from knitted stitches. Crochet stitches are taller: A single crochet stitch equals about two knit rows, a half double crochet equals about three knit rows, and a double crochet equals about four knit rows. The width isn't a direct conversion either, but it varies greatly depending on the weight of the yarn and the size of the hooks and needles used. For example, if you begin a knit garment by casting on 70 stitches on a size 6 needle, you can't simply convert to crochet by chaining 70 stitches on a size 6 hook. The crochet piece will end up wider. Add to the mix increasing and decreasing for shaping armholes, necklines, etc., and the complexity really deepens. The crochet piece will be heavier and use more yarn than its knitted counterpart, so that is another consideration.

I am not saying that it cannot be done. With the help of a calculator, knowledge of lots of different stitches and how they behave, the ability to convert gauge and figure out how many crochet stitches it would take to get the same size swatch as a knitted piece, and understanding the slope of decreasing or increasing, you could probably do it. Do you have that much patience? It is not just a matter of substituting the same amount of crochet stitches for knit stitches, but writing a whole new set of instructions, and it certainly is not for beginners. In essence, it means designing an entirely new pattern in knit or crochet to mimic a similar pattern done in the other medium.

Nevertheless, I was thoroughly intrigued by the whole concept, so I decided to play around a little. I made swatch after swatch, using many different weight yarns and different size needles and hooks. It was a huge learning experience for me, even with all my years of knitting and crocheting. As I was playing around with the different stitches in both knit and crochet, I decided to see if I could make something that looked the same in both mediums. I found that while you can get a comparable item, you cannot get an exact copy. I found many stitches that did look alike in both knit and crochet, but the gauge was still different in most cases. In very few instances, I could achieve the same look and the same gauge. I must admit, I really enjoyed the process!

Putting all my experimentation to good use, I've written this book of patterns, providing instructions for each item in both knit and crochet. Are you a die-hard knitter, a passionate crochet fan, or someone who enjoys both? Now you have a choice. I've done all the calculations and trial swatches for you. You simply need to decide whether you want to knit or crochet each project. Knit it the first time and crochet it the second time (or vice versa). For each project pair, I explain how the yarn and gauge behaves and how I achieved the similar looks in the knit and crochet versions. Once you've finished a few projects, you may choose to use the stitch patterns to do a little converting of your own. I hope that you enjoy the book and learn a few new tricks along the way.

Margaret

wooden handle tote

If you thought only knitters could cable, think again! Knitters cable by working stitches out of order. In crochet, a similar effect is achieved with front post double crochet stitches that cross. The great crescent shape of these roomy handbags is achieved by simply gathering the edges of a rectangle—clever and uncomplicated. Twisted cord ties at the base of the handles hold the two sides together. Both totes are made with smooth cotton yarn that shows off the cables very well. To make them durable and useful, the bags are interlined with fleece and lined with cotton fabric.

Wooden Handle Tote knit

YARN

Medium-weight
smooth yarn

Shown: *Cotton Ease* by Lion Brand,
50% cotton, 50% acrylic, 3.5 oz.
(100 g)/207 yd. (186 m): terracotta
#134, 3 skeins

NEEDLES

Size 8 (5 mm) or size to
obtain correct gauge
Two cable needles

STITCHES

Knit
Purl

GAUGE

18 sts = 4" (10 cm)
Take time to check gauge.

NOTIONS/SUPPLIES

Tapestry needle
Pair of handles, 7⅞" (20 cm)
wide at the base
Shown: Purse-n-alize-it! twisted
bamboo handles
½ yd. (0.5 m) fleece interfacing
½ yd. (0.5 m) lining fabric
Sewing needle and thread

SIZE

17" x 26" (43 x 66 cm)
before assembly

Tote Body

*Note: The first stitch of every row
is slipped to give the edge a more
finished appearance.*

Cast on 77 sts.

Rows 1, 3, 5 (RS): Sl1, k1, yo,
k2tog, k to last 4 sts, k2tog, yo, k2.

Rows 2, 4, 6: Sl1, k across row.

Row 7: Sl1, k1, yo, k2tog, *p8, k1,
p3, k1, rep from * once, p17, **k1,
p3, k1, p8, rep from ** once, end
k2tog, yo, k2.

Row 8: K4, *k8, p1, k3, p1, rep
from * once, k17, **p1, k3, p1, k8,
rep from ** once, end k4.

Row 9: Sl1, k3, *p8, k1, p3, k1,
rep from * once, p17, ** k1, p3,
k1, p8, rep from ** once, end k4.

Rows 10, 12, and 14: Rep Row 8.

Row 11: Rep Row 7.

Row 13 (cable twist row): Sl1, k3,
*p8, [sl next st to CN and hold to
front of work, sl next 3 sts to 2nd

CN, hold to back of work, k next st
from left-hand needle, p3 from 2nd
CN, then k st from first CN], rep
from * once, p17, rep bet [ ]s once,
p8, rep bet [ ]s once, p8, k4.

Rep Rows 7–14 for patt until piece
measures 26" (66 cm). Bind off.

Twisted Cord

Make 2.

Cut two strands of yarn, each 4½
yd. (4 m), hold together, fold in
half. Anchor the folded end, twist
these strands until they become
very tightly wound. Being sure not
to release ends, bring cut ends and
folded ends together, hold up and
allow to twist into a cord. Tie the
loose side tightly, about 1½" (4 cm)
from end, to form a small tassel
and to anchor cord. Make a second
cord. Set cords aside to be used to
form top of bag.

Lining

Line bag while flat before assembly.

Cut the fleece interfacing so it does not cover the eyelet edges formed by the yarn-over stitches. Hand-sew in place. Cut the lining fabric 1" (2.5 cm) larger than the fleece. Fold under all sides ½" (1.3 cm). Sew the lining to the bag, over the interfacing.

Finishing

Using a large safety pin, weave the finished cords in and out of the eyelet holes at edges of bag; draw up tightly.

Using leftover purse yarn and a tapestry needle, sew the handles to the top corners of the bag.

Tie opposite cord ends together in bows at the base of the handles.

Wooden Handle Tote
crochet

YARN
Medium-weight
smooth yarn
Shown: *Cotton-Ease* by Lion
Brand, 50% cotton, 50% acrylic,
3.5 oz. (100 g)/207 yd. (186 m):
terracotta #134, 3 skeins

HOOKS
Size G-6 (4 mm) or size to
obtain correct gauge

STITCHES
Chain stitch
Single crochet
Front post double crochet

GAUGE
13½ sts = 4" (10 cm)
Take time to check gauge.

NOTIONS/SUPPLIES
Tapestry needle
Pair of handles, 7⅞" (20 cm)
wide at the base
Shown: Purse-n-alize-it! twisted
bamboo handles
½ yd. (0.5 m) fleece interfacing
½ yd. (0.5 m) lining fabric
Sewing needle and thread

SIZE
17" x 26" (43 x 66 cm)
before assembly

Tote body

Notes:
1. The beg ch 1 counts as a sc and will be referred to as sc throughout.
2. Front post double crochet (FPdc): Yarn over, insert hook from front to back to front again around the post of next st, yo, draw yarn through st, (yo, draw yarn through 2 loops on hook) twice.

Ch 59.

Foundation row: Working in the BL of each ch, starting in 2nd ch from hook, work 1 sc in each ch across row, turn—58 sc.

Row 1 (eyelet row) (RS): Ch 1 (counts as a sc now and through-out), sk first sc, working in the BL only, sc in next sc, ch 1, sk next sc, 1 sc in each sc across to within last 3 sc, ch 1, sk next sc, 1 sc in next sc, sc in top of tch, turn.

Row 2: Working in BL only, ch 1, sk first sc, 1 sc in next sc, 1 sc in next ch-1 space, 1 sc in each sc across to next ch-1 space, 1 sc in next ch-1 space, 1 sc in each of the last 2 sts, turn.

Rows 3–4: Rep Rows 1–2.

Row 5 (begin cable pat): Ch 1, sk first sc, working in BL only, 1 sc in next sc, ch 1, sk next sc, 1 sc in next sc, *working in both loops of sts, 1 sc in each of the next 6 sc, FPdc around the post of next st, 1 sc next sc, FPdc around the post of next st; rep from * once, 1 sc in each of next 14 sc, **FPdc around the post of next st, sc in next st, FPdc around the post of next st, 1 sc in each of next 6; rep from ** once, working in BL only, 1 sc in next sc, ch 1, sk next sc, 1 sc in each of last 2 sts, turn.

Row 6: Ch 1, sk first sc, working in BL only, 1 sc in next sc, 1 sc in next ch-1 sp, 1 sc in next sc, working in both loops of sts, 1 sc in each st across to within last 4 sts, working in BL only, 1 sc in next sc, 1 sc in next ch-1 sp, 1 sc in each of last 2 sts, turn.

Row 7: Ch 1, sk first sc, working in BL only, 1 sc in next sc, ch 1, sk next sc, 1 sc in next sc, *working in both loops of sts, 1 sc in each of next 6 sc, FPdc around the post of next FPdc, 1 sc in next sc, FPdc around the post of next FPdc; rep from * once, 1 sc in each of next

14 sc, **FPdc around the post of next FPdc, 1 sc in next sc, FPdc around the post of next FPdc, 1 sc in each of the next 6 sc; rep from ** once, working in BL only, 1 sc in next sc, ch 1, sk next sc, 1 sc in each of last 2 sts, turn.

Row 8: Rep Row 6.

Row 9: Ch 1, sk first sc, working in BL only, 1 sc in next sc, ch 1, sk next sc, 1 sc in next sc, *working in both loops of sts, sc in each of next 6 sc, sk next FPdc and next sc, FPdc around the post of next FPdc, 1 sc in skipped sc, FPdc around the

post of last skipped FPdc (cable twist made) rep from * once, 1 sc in each of next 14 sc, **sk over next FPdc and next sc, FPdc around the post of next FPdc, 1 sc in skipped sc, FPdc around the post of last skipped FPdc, 1 sc in each of next 6 sc; rep from ** once, working in BL only, 1 sc in next sc, ch 1, sk next sc, 1 sc in each of last 2 sts, turn.

Rows 10–11: Rep Rows 6–7.

Rep Rows 6–11 until piece measures 25" (63.5 cm) from beg, then rep Rows 2–3 twice. End off.

Finishing

Make the cord, line the rectangle, and finish the bag following the directions on pages 10 and 11 for the knitted bag.

Luxury scarf

Take a well-loved stitch, add a gorgeous yarn with standout colors, and wrap yourself in this luxuriously long, extra-wide scarf. The stitches used in both the knit and crochet versions are fairly easy, the knit being a four-row repeat, the crochet a one-row repeat.

To create these knit and crochet look-alikes, I made several swatches and calculated carefully. Even though I used the same yarn and same size hook and needle, in order to get the same width, I had to increase the number of stitches for the knitted version.

Luxury Scarf
Knit

YARN
Superfine yarn

1 SUPER FINE

Shown: *Kureyon Sock Yarn* by Noro, 70% wool, 30% nylon, 3.5 oz. (100 g)/459 yd. (413 m): color S188, 2 skeins

NEEDLES
Size 6 (4 mm) or size to obtain correct gauge

STITCHES
Knit
Purl

GAUGE
27½ sts = 4" (10 cm) in pattern stitch
Take time to check gauge.

NOTIONS/SUPPLIES
Tapestry needle

SIZE
16" x 60" (40.5 x 152.5 cm)

Scarf

Cast on 110 sts.

Row 1: Knit.

Row 2: K1, purl to last st, k1.

Row 3: K1, (yo, k1) 3 times, *(k2tog) 6 times, (yo, k1) 6 times, rep from * 5 times more, end (yo, k1) 3 times, k1.

Row 4: Knit.

Rep Rows 1–4 until 60" (152.5 cm), end with Row 4. Bind off in knit.

Finishing

Weave in loose ends.

To block, lay scarf on a towel, folded in half. Spritz with water, pat into shape, and allow to dry.

Luxury Scarf — crochet

YARN

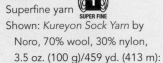

Superfine yarn
Shown: *Kureyon Sock Yarn* by
Noro, 70% wool, 30% nylon,
3.5 oz. (100 g)/459 yd. (413 m):
color S188: 3 skeins

HOOKS

Size G-6 (4 mm) or size to
obtain correct gauge

STITCHES

Chain stitch
Slip stitch
Double crochet

GAUGE

14 sts (one patt repeat) = 3"
(7.5 cm) in chevron pattern
Take time to check gauge.

NOTIONS/SUPPLIES

Tapestry needle

SIZE

17½" x 60" (44.5 x 152.5 cm)

Scarf

*Note: Dc3tog: (yo, insert hook in
next st, yo, draw yarn through
st, yo, draw yarn through 2 loops
on hook) 3 times, yo, draw yarn
through 4 loops on hook.*

Ch 87.

Foundation row: 2 dc in 3rd ch
from hook, *1 dc in each of the
next 3 ch, (dc3tog in next 3 ch) 2
times, 1 dc in each of the next 3 ch
3 dc in each of next 2 ch; rep from
* 4 times more, 1 dc in each of the
next 3 ch, (dc3tog in next 3 ch) 2
times, 1 dc in each of next 3 ch, 3
dc in last ch, turn.

Row 1: Ch 3 (counts as first dc), 2
dc in the first dc, *1 dc in each of
the next 3 dc, (dc3tog in next 3 dc)
2 times, 1 dc in each of the next 3
dc, 3 dc in each of next 2 dc; rep
from * 4 times more, 1 dc in each
of the next 3 ch, (dc3tog in next 3
sts) 2 times, 1 dc in each of the next
3 ch, 3 dc in top of tch, turn.

Rep Row 1 until scarf measures
60" (152.5 cm) from beg. End off.

Finishing

Weave in loose ends.

To block, lay scarf on a towel,
folded in half. Spritz with water,
pat into shape, and allow to dry.

cozy slippers

These cozy slippers are made using two strands of yarn held together. The double strand gives the slippers extra body and warmth. I embellished them with a contrasting color yarn for the ruffle and flowers. It is interesting that I got the same stitch count per row but, as in most cases, the crochet stitch was taller than the knit stitch. There are two knitted rows to every crocheted row. You can eliminate the flowers and ruffle and make slippers for boys or men. Take care when wearing these slippers on slippery floors, such as tile or wood. I guess that's why they're called slippers!

Cozy Slippers

knit

YARN

Medium-weight
smooth yarn
Shown: *Décor* by Patons,
75% acrylic, 25% wool, 3.5 oz.
(100 g)/210 yd. (189 m):
woodbine ombre #16231 (MC),
2 skeins; taupe #1631 (CC),
1 skein

NEEDLES

Size 9 (5.5 mm) or size to
obtain correct gauge

STITCHES

Garter stitch (knit every row)

GAUGE

14 sts = 4" (10 cm)
Take time to check gauge.

NOTIONS/SUPPLIES

Tapestry needle

SIZE

Small (Medium, Large)
Finished size: 9½" (24 cm) long
x 6" (15 cm) tall (10" [25.5 cm]
long x 6½" [16.5 cm] tall, 10½"
[26.5 cm] long x 7" [18 cm] tall)

Slipper

Note: Yarn is double-stranded throughout.

Make 2.

Starting at bottom, with MC, cast on 66 (74, 82) sts. Knit every row for 14 (16, 18) rows.

Next row (first dec row): K30 (34, 38), sl1, k1, psso, p2, k2tog, k30 (34, 38)—64 (72, 80) sts.

Next row (second dec row): K29 (33, 37), sl1, k1, psso, k2, k2tog, k29 (33, 37)—62 (70, 78) sts.

Next row (third dec row): K28 (32, 36) sl1, k1, psso, p2, k2tog, k28 (32, 36)—60 (68, 76) sts.

Next row (fourth dec row): K27 (31, 35) sl1, k1, psso, k2, k2tog, k27 (31, 35)—58 (66, 74) sts.

Cont in this manner, keeping the center 2 sts in St st (1 row knit, 1 row purl), with all other sts in garter st (knit every row); at the same time, dec 1 st before and after the 2 center sts until there are 34 (38, 42) sts on needle.

Work garter st on all sts for 5 (6, 7) rows more.

Cuff

K17 (19, 21) sts, place rem 17 (19, 21) sts on holder to be worked later for second half of cuff. Cont in garter st on 17 (19, 21) sts for 12 (14, 16) more rows. Bind off in knit.

Join yarn at center of slipper, place 17 (19, 21) sts from holder onto knitting needle, finish to correspond to other side.

Sew back and sole seam.

Ruffle

Using single strand of CC yarn, with right side facing you, starting in first bound-off st of cuff, pick up 1 st in each bound-off st—34 (38, 42) sts.

Row 1: Knit across row, inc 1 st every other st—51 (57, 63) sts.

Row 2: Knit.

Row 3: Knit across row, inc 1 st every st—102 (114, 126) sts.

Row 4: Knit.

Row 5: Knit across row, inc 1 st every other st—153 (171, 189) sts.

Bind off in knit.

Flower

Make 4 (2 per slipper).

Using single strand of CC, cast on 62 sts.

Row 1 (WS): Purl.

Row 2: K2, *k1, sl this st back onto left needle, then lift the next 9 sts on left needle over this st and off the needle, yo, knit the first st again, k2, rep from * 4 times more—22 sts.

Row 3: P1, *p2tog, k front, back, front of the space created by the yo, p1, rep from * to last st, p1—27 sts.

Row 4: K1, *sl2, k1, p2sso, rep from * 7 times, end k2tog—10 sts.

Row 5: *P2tog, rep from *—5 sts. End off leaving a 10" (25.5 cm) length of yarn, thread on a tapestry needle, draw through rem sts. Sew last petal to first petal to form flower.

Finishing

Stack two flowers and sew together; sew in place on slipper.

No blocking required.

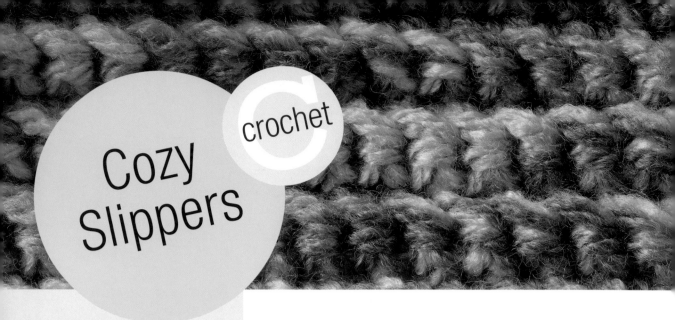

Cozy Slippers

crochet

YARN

Medium-weight
smooth yarn

Shown: *Décor* by Patons, 75% acrylic, 25% wool, 3.5 oz. (100 g)/210 yd. (189 m): woodbine ombre #16231 (MC), 2 skeins; taupe #1631 (CC), 1 skein

HOOKS

Size I-9 (5.5 mm) or size to obtain correct gauge

STITCHES

Chain stitch
Slip stitch
Single crochet
Double crochet
Triple crochet
Front post double crochet
Back post double crochet

GAUGE

14 sts = 4" (10 cm)
Take time to check gauge.

NOTIONS/SUPPLIES

Tapestry needle
Stitch markers or scrap yarn for markers

SIZE

Small (Medium, Large)
Finished size: 9½" (24 cm) long x 6" (15 cm) tall (10" [25.5 cm] long x 6½" [16.5 cm] tall, 10½" [26.5 cm] long x 7" [18 cm] tall)

Slippers

Notes:

1. Single crochet always worked through BL (except for ruffle and flower).

2. Yarn is used double-stranded throughout.

3. Sc2tog: Insert hook in next st, yo, draw yarn through st, insert hook in next st, yo, draw yarn through st, yo, draw yarn through 3 loops on hook.

4. Front post double crochet (FPdc): Yarn over, insert hook from front to back to front again around the post of next st, yo, draw yarn through st, (yo, draw yarn through 2 loops on hook) twice.

5. Back post double crochet (BPdc): Yarn over, insert hook from back to front to front again around the post of next st, yo, draw yarn through st, (yo, draw yarn through 2 loops on hook) twice.

Make 2.

Starting at bottom, with 2 strands of MC, ch 67 (75, 83).

Foundation row: Starting in 2nd ch from hook, work 1 sc in each ch across, turn—66 (74, 82) sc.

Row 1: Ch 1 (counts as first sc), sk first st, 1 sc in BL of next 64 (72, 80) sc, sc in top of tch, turn—66 (74, 82) sts.

Row 2: Ch 1 (counts as first sc), sk first st, 1 sc in BL of each st across, sc in top of tch, turn—66 (74, 82) sts.

Rep Row 2 for 5 (6, 7) more rows.

Shape Arch

Row 1 (RS): Place a marker between center 2 sts, move marker up as work progresses. Ch 1 (counts as first sc), sk first st, sc in each st across to within 3 sts before marker, sc2tog in next 2 sts, FPdc around the post of next 2 sts, sc2tog in next 2 sts, sc in each st across, 1 sc in top of tch, turn—64 (72, 80) sts.

Row 2 (WS): Ch 1 (counts as first sc), sk first st 1 sc in each st across to within 3 sts before marker, sc2tog in next 2 sts, BPdc around the post of next 2 sts, sc2tog in next 2 sts, sc in each st across, 1 sc in top of tch, turn—62 (70, 78) sts.

Rows 3–4: Rep Rows 1–2—58 (66, 74) sts at end of last row.

Row 5 (RS): Ch 1 (counts as first sc), sk first st, sc in each st across to within 5 sts before marker, (sc2tog in next 2 sts) twice, FPdc around the post of next 2 sts, (sc2tog in next 2 sts) twice, sc in each st across, 1 sc in top of tch, turn—54 (62, 70) sts.

Row 6 (WS): Ch 1 (counts as first sc), sk first st, sc in each st across to within 5 sts before marker, (sc2tog in next 2 sts) twice, BPdc around the post of next 2 sts, (sc2tog in next 2 sts) twice, sc in each st across, 1 sc in top of turning ch, turn—50 (58, 66) sts.

Rows 7–8: Rep Rows 5–6—42 (50, 58) sts at end of last row.

First Side of Cuff

Row 1: Ch 1 (counts as first sc), sk first st, working in BL of sts, sc next 16 (20, 24), sc2tog in next 2 sts, turn, leaving rem sts unworked (to be worked later for other side of cuff). Work even in sc in BL patt on 18 (22, 26) sts as established for 7 (8, 9) rows. End off.

Second Side of Cuff

Row 1: Sk 4 sts to the left of last st made in Row 1 of First Side of Cuff, join MC in BL of next sc, ch 1 (counts as first sc), sk first st, work-

ing in BL of sts, sc2tog in next 2 sts, sc in each sc across, sc in top of tch, turn. Work even in sc in BL patt on 18 (22, 26) sts as established for 7 (8, 9) rows. End off.

With MC, sew back and sole seam.

Ruffle

Use a single strand of CC.

Row 1: With RS facing, starting in first st at top of cuff, ch 1 (counts as first sc), sk first st, 2 sc in next st, *1 sc in next st, 2 sc in next st; rep from * across, ending with 2 sc in top of tch, turn—54 (66, 78) sts.

Row 2: Ch 1 (counts as first sc), 1 sc in first st, 2 sc in each st across, ending with 2 sc in top of tch, turn—108 (132, 156) sts.

Row 3: Rep Row 1—162 (198, 234) sts. End off.

Flower

Make 4 (2 per slipper).

Using single strand of CC, ch 5, join with sl st to form a ring.

Rnd 1: Ch 1, 10 sc in ring, sl st in first sc to join.

Rnd 2: *Ch 3, 3 tr in next st, ch 3, sl st in next st; rep from *4 times more (5 petals), sl st in first sl st to join. End off.

Stack 2 flowers and sew together in center; sew to center top of slipper.

No blocking required.

Lady's Lacy cardigan

One of the most delicate patterns in crochet is the shell stitch, and there are many variations to choose from. Crocheted shells are created by hooking multiple stitches—in this case triple and double triple crochets—into the same stitch. The crocheted jacket is worked from the top down so the shells fan downward. Knitted shells are created by making multiple yarnovers in one row and then working them together in the following row. The knitted version is worked from the bottom up, to make the shells fan in the same direction as the crocheted version. The pattern is a little tricky, so have patience and practice before you begin. The results are gorgeous!

Lady's Lacy Cardigan

Knit

YARN

DK weight yarn

Shown: *Baby Alpaca DK* by Plymouth Yarn, 100% baby alpaca, 1.8 oz. (50 g)/125 yd. (113 m): red violet #4818, 8 (8, 9) skeins

NEEDLES

Size 5 (3.75 mm)

Size 6 (4 mm) or sizes to obtain correct gauge

STITCHES

Knitted shell stitch

Garter stitch

Reverse stockinette stitch

GAUGE

1 shell = 2½" (6.5 cm)

Take time to check gauge.

NOTIONS/SUPPLIES

Stitch markers

Stitch holders

Tapestry needle

1" (2.5 cm) button

SIZE

Small (Medium, Large)

Finished chest size: 34 (36, 38)" [86.5 (91.5, 96.5) cm]

Jacket

Notes:

1. Pay close attention to the yarn-over placement. On some rows you will be making only one stitch in the stitch that is made by the yarnover; on other rows, you will be making more than one stitch in the made stitch.

2. Row stitch count changes on some rows because of the made stitches.

3. To make a yarnover for this pattern, wrap yarn around needle twice to the front. This is necessary to form the yarnovers from the purl sides.

4. To keep a nice even edge, slip the first stitch of every row, and knit the last stitch of every row, from the back loop.

5. Jacket is worked from the bottom up.

Pattern Stitch

Multiple of 19 sts.

Rows 1 and 2: Knit.

Row 3: *K1, yo, p2tog, k13, p2tog, yo, k1, rep from * across.

Row 4: *K1 (k1, p1) into st made by the yo, k15, (p1, k1) into made st, k1, rep from * across.

Rows 5 and 6: Knit.

Row 7: *K1, (yo, p2tog) twice, k11, (p2tog, yo) twice, k1, rep from * across.

Row 8: *[K1, (k1, p1), into made st] twice, k13, [(p1, k1) into made st, k1] twice, rep from * across.

Row 9: Knit.

Row 10: *K6, (yo, k1) 14 times, k5, rep from * across.

Row 11: *K1, (yo, p2tog) twice, yo, sl next 15 sts to right-hand needle, allowing all wraps to drop forming long sts, then sl all long sts back on the left-hand needle and purl them all tog forming shell, (yo, p2tog) twice, yo, k1, rep from * across.

Row 12: *[K1, (p1, k1) into made st] 3 times, k1, [(k 1, p 1) into made st, k1] 3 times, rep from * across.

Rep Rows 1–12 for patt.

Back

With size 6 needles, cast on 80 (86, 92) sts. Keeping 2 (5, 8) sts each side in garter st (knit every row), work 12 patt rows on the 76 center sts, until 11½ (12, 12½)" [29, (30.5, 32) cm] from beg. Place marker in work at each side to mark sleeve placement.

Cont working in patt until Back is 18½ (19½, 20½)" [47 (49.5, 52) cm] from beg.

Work 4 rows garter st. At beg of next 2 rows, bind off 20 (22, 24) sts. Place rem 40 (42, 44) sts on holder to be worked later.

Left Front

With size 6 needles, cast on 45 (48, 51) sts.

Row 1: K2 (5, 8) sts, place marker on needle, work Patt Row 1 on next 38 sts, place marker on needle, k last 5 sts (this will be front border).

Row 2: K5, work Patt Row 2 on next 38 sts, k last 2 (5, 8) sts.

Cont in this manner, keeping 5 sts at front edge and 2 (5, 8) sts at arm edge in garter st, working patt rows

in center until 11½ (12, 12½)" [29 (30.5, 32) cm] from beg.

Place marker at arm side for Sleeve placement.

Cont as established until approximately 16 (17, 18)" [40.5 (43, 45.5) cm] from beg, ending with Row 12 of patt.

At neck edge (beg of next WS row), bind off 20 (21, 22) sts. Cont to keep patt as established, dec 1 st neck edge every row 5 times. Work even on rem 20 (22, 24) sts until 18½ (19½, 20½)" [47 (49.5, 52) cm] from beg. Work garter st for 4 rows. Bind off.

Right Front

Work same as Left Front, marking arm side for Sleeve placement and reversing neck shaping.

Sleeves

Make 2.

With size 6 needles, cast on 42 (44, 46) sts.

Row 1: K2 (3, 4) place marker on needle, work Patt Row 1 on next 38 sts, place marker on needle, k2 (3, 4) sts. Work in patt, keeping sts outside marker in garter st as sts are increased, inc 1 st each side every 6th row 24 (26, 28) times—90 (96, 102) sts.

Work even as established until sleeve measures 15½ (16, 16½)" [39.5 (40.5, 42) cm] from beg. Work garter st for 4 rows. Bind off.

Sew shoulder seams.

(continued)

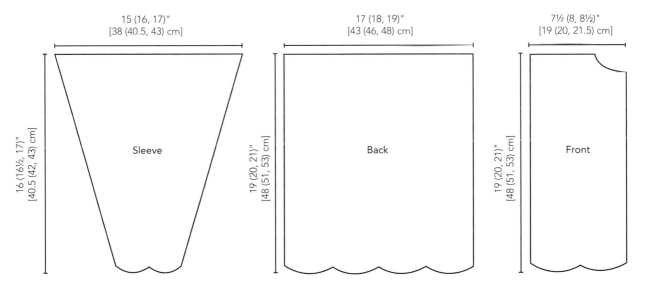

15 (16, 17)"
[38 (40.5, 43) cm]

16 (16½, 17)"
[40.5 (42, 43) cm]

Sleeve

17 (18, 19)"
[43 (46, 48) cm]

19 (20, 21)"
[48 (51, 53) cm]

Back

7½ (8, 8½)"
[19 (20, 21.5) cm]

19 (20, 21)"
[48 (51, 53) cm]

Front

Lady's Lacy Cardigan (continued)

Neckband

Starting at top Right Front edge, with right side facing you, using size 5 needles, pick up and k20 (20, 20) along bound off sts at neck edge, pick up 3 sts along right front shaped edge, k40 (42, 44) sts from Back holder, pick up 3 sts along left front shaped edge, pick up and k20 (20, 20) sts in bound off sts of Left Front—86 (88, 90) sts.

Row 1 (WS): Knit.

Row 2: K1, bind off next 3 sts (beg of buttonhole), k across row.

Row 3: Knit to bound off sts, cast on 3 sts (buttonhole completed), k1.

Row 4: Knit.

Row 5: Knit.

Bind off using picot bind-off as follows:

Bind off first 2 sts, *turn, using cable cast on, cast on 2 additional sts, turn work, pass second st over the first, then third over the first (1 st rem on needle), bind off 2 more sts, rep from * until all sts are bound off.

Finishing

Mark center of Sleeve. Pin Sleeve in place, centering on shoulder and ending at markers. Sew Sleeve in place. Sew underarm and side seams. Sew on button.

Blocking: Place on a padded surface, such as several towels, spritz with water till garment is wet but not saturated. Pat into shape, pinning if necessary (be sure to use rustproof pins), place a second towel on top, allow to dry.

Lady's Lacy Cardigan
crochet

YARN

DK weight yarn

Shown: *Baby Alpaca DK* by
   Plymouth Yarn, 100% baby
   alpaca, 1.8 oz. (50 g)/125 yd.
   (113 m): red violet #4818:
   9 (9, 10) skeins

HOOKS

Size G-6 (4 mm)
Size H-8 (5 mm) or sizes to
   obtain correct gauge

STITCHES

Single crochet
Triple crochet
Double triple crochet
Front post triple crochet
Back post triple crochet

GAUGE

One pattern repeat of 16 sts
(1 shell plus 5 post tr) = 4" (10 cm)
Take time to check gauge.

NOTIONS/SUPPLIES

Tapestry needle

SIZE

Small (Medium, Large)
Finished chest size: 34 (36, 38)"
   [86.5 (91.5, 96.5) cm]
Length: 19 (20, 21)"
   [48.5 (51, 53.5) cm]

Notes:
*1. Triple crochet (tr): Yarn over
2 times, insert hook in next st,
[yo and draw through 2 loops on
hook] 3 times.*

*2. Double triple crochet (dtr): Yarn
over 3 times, insert hook in next st
[yo and draw through 2 loops on
hook] 4 times.*

*3. Front post triple crochet (FPtr):
Yarn over twice, insert hook from
front to back to front again around
the post of next st, yo, draw yarn
through st, [yo, draw yarn through
2 loops on hook] 3 times.*

*4. Back post triple crochet (BPtr):
Yarn over twice, insert hook from
back to front to back again around
the post of next st, yo, draw yarn
through st, [yo, draw yarn through
2 loops on hook] 3 times.*

*5. Tr2tog (triple crochet decrease):
Yarn over twice, insert hook in next
st, yo, draw through st, [yo, draw
through 2 loops on hook] twice, yo
twice, insert hook in next st, yo,
draw through st, [yo, draw through
2 loops on hook] twice, yo, draw
through 3 loops on hook.*

*6. Jacket is worked from the top
to the bottom.*

Back

Starting at top with larger hook,
ch 73 (77, 81).

Foundation row: Starting in 2nd ch
from hook, work 1 sc in each ch
across row, turn—72 (76, 80) sc.

Row 1 (RS): Ch 1 (counts as first
sc), sk first sc, 1 sc in each of next
70 (74, 78) sc, sc in top of tch,
turn—72 (76, 80) sts.

Row 2: Ch 3 (counts as first tr), sk
first sc, 1 tr in each of the next 5 (7,
9) sc, *sk next 5 sc, 11 dtr in next
sc, sk next 5 sc, 1 tr in each of the
next 5 sc; rep from * 3 times more,
1 tr in each of next 0 (2, 4) sc, 1 tr
in top of tch, turn.

Row 3: Ch 3 (counts as first tr), sk
first st, 1 FPtr in each of next 5 (7,
9) sts,*sk next 5 dtr, 11 dtr in next
dtr (center of shell), sk next 5 dtr,
1 FPtr in each of the next 5 sts; rep
from * 3 times more, FPtr in each
of next 0 (2, 4) sts, 1 tr in top of
tch, turn.

Row 4: Ch 3 (counts as first tr), sk
first st, 1 BPtr in each of next 5 (7,
9) sts, *sk next 5 dtr, 11 dtr in next
dtr (center of shell), sk next 5 dtr, 1
BPtr each of next 5 sts; rep from *
3 times more, BPtr in each of next
0 (2, 4) sts, 1 tr in top of tch, turn.

Rep Rows 3–4 until piece measures
19 (20, 21)" [48.5 (51, 53.5) cm],
measuring from top edge to bottom
of shell in last row. End off. Place
a marker 7½ (8, 8½)" [19 (20.5,
21.5) cm] below shoulder for Sleeve
placement.

Lady's Lacy Cardigan (continued)

Left Front

Starting at top with larger hook, ch 21 (23, 25).

Foundation row: Starting in 2nd ch from hook, work 1 sc in each ch across, turn—20 (22, 24) sc.

Row 1 (RS): Ch 1 (counts as first sc), sk first sc, 1 sc in each of next 18 (20, 22) sc, 1 sc in top of tch, turn—20 (22, 24) sts.

Row 2: Ch 3 (counts as first tr), sk the first sc, 1 tr in each of next 5 (7, 9) sc, *sk next 5 sc, 11 dtr in next sc, sk next 5 sc, 1 tr in each of the next 3 sc, ch 19 (21, 23) at end of row, turn. (This added ch forms neckline.)

Row 3: Working on the new added ch, starting in 6th ch from hook (5 skipped ch sts count as first tr), work 1 tr in each of next 1 (3, 5) ch, sk next 5 ch, 11 dtr in next ch, sk next 5 ch, 1 tr in each of next 2 ch, 1 FPtr in each of next 3 tr, sk next 5 dtr, 11 dtr in next dtr (center of shell), sk next 5 dtr, 1 FPtr in each of next 5 (7, 9) tr, 1 tr in top of tch, turn.

Row 4: Ch 3 (counts as first tr), sk first st, 1 BPtr in each of next 5 (7, 9) sts, *sk next 5 dtr, 11 dtr in next dtr (center of shell), sk next 5 dtr, 1 BPtr each of next 5 sts; rep from * 3 times more, BPtr in each of next 0 (2, 4) sts, 1 tr in top of tch, turn.

Row 5: Ch 3 (counts as first tr), 1 FPtr in each of next 1 (3, 5) sts, sk next 5 dtr, 11 dtr in next dtr (center of shell), sk next 5 dtr, 1 FPtr in each of next 5 sts, sk next 5 dtr, 11 dtr in next dtr (center of shell), sk next 5 dtr, 1 FPtr in each of next 5 (7, 9) sts, 1 tr in top of tch, turn.

Rep Rows 4–5 until piece measures same as finished Back. End off. Place a marker 7½ (8, 8½)" [19 (20.5, 21.5) cm] below shoulder on side edge for Sleeve placement.

Right Front

Starting at top with larger hook, ch 21 (23, 25).

Foundation row: Starting in 2nd ch from hook, work 1 sc in each ch across row, turn—20 (22, 24) sc.

Row 1 (WS): Ch 1 (counts as first sc), sk first sc, 1 sc in each of next 18 (20, 22) sc, sc in top of tch, turn—20 (22, 24) sts.

Row 2: Ch 3 (counts as first tr), sk first sc, 1 tr in each of the next 5 (7, 9) sc, *sk next 5 sc, 11 dtr in next sc, sk next 5 sc, 1 tr in each of the next 3 sc, ch 19 (21, 23) at end of row, turn. (This added ch forms neckline.)

Row 3: Working on the new added ch, starting in 6th ch from hook (5 skipped ch sts count as first tr), work 1 tr in each of next 1 (3, 5) ch, sk next 5 ch, 11 dtr in next ch, sk next 5 ch, 1 tr in each of next 2 ch, 1 BPtr in each of next 3 tr, sk next 5 dtr, 11 dtr in next dtr (center of shell), sk next 5 dtr, 1 BPtr in each of next 5 (7, 9) tr, 1 tr in top of tch, turn.

Row 4: Ch 3 (counts as first tr), sk first st, 1 FPtr in each of next 5 (7, 9) sts, *sk next 5 dtr, 11 dtr in next dtr (center of shell), sk next 5 dtr, 11 FPtr each of next 5 sts; rep from * 3 times more, FPtr in each of next 0 (2, 4) sts, 1 tr in top of tch, turn.

Row 5: Ch 3 (counts as first tr), 1 BPtr in each of next 1 (3, 5) sts, sk next 5 dtr, 11 dtr in next dtr (center of shell), sk next 5 dtr, 1 BPtr in each of next 5 sts, sk next 5 dtr, 11 dtr in next dtr (center of shell), sk next 5 dtr, 1 BPtr in each of next 5 (7, 9) sts, 1 tr in top of tch, turn.

Rep Rows 4–5 until piece measures same as finished Back. End off. Place a marker 7½ (8, 8½)" [19 (20.5, 21.5) cm] below shoulder on side edge for Sleeve placement.

Sleeves

Starting at top with larger hook, ch 60 (64, 68).

Foundation row: Starting in 2nd ch from hook, work 1 sc in each ch across, turn—59 (63, 67) sc.

Row 1: Ch 1 (counts as first sc), sk first sc, sc in each of next 57 (61, 65) sc, sc in top of tch, turn—59 (63, 67) sts.

Change to smaller hook.

Row 2: Ch 3 (cts as first tr), sk first sc, 1 tr in each of next 15 (17, 19) sc, sk next 5 sc, 11 dtr in next sc, sk next 5 sc, 1 tr in each of next 5 sc, sk next 5 sc, 11 dtr in next sc, sk next 5 sc, 1 tr in each of next 15 (17, 19) sc, 1 tr in top of tch, turn—2 shells, 5 tr center, 16 (18, 20) tr on each side.

Row 3: Ch 3 (counts as first tr), sk first tr, 1 tr in each of next 15 (17, 19) sts, *sk next 5 dtr, 11 dtr in next dtr (center of shell), sk next 5 dtr*, 1 FPtr in each of next 5 sts; rep from * to * once, end 1 tr in each of next 15 (17, 19) sts, 1 tr in top of tch, turn.

Row 4: Ch 3 (counts as first tr), sk first tr, 1 tr in each of the next 15 (17, 19) sts, *sk 5 dtr, 11 dtr in next dtr (center of shell), sk next 5 dtr*, 1 BPtr in each of next 5 sts; rep from * to * once, end 1 tr in each of next 15 (17, 19) sts, 1 tr in top of tch, turn.

Rep Rows 3–4, dec 1 st by working tr2tog at each end of every 3rd row 10 times. When dec are complete there will be 6 (8, 10) tr on either side of shells. Maintaining patt as established, work even on rem sts until sleeve measures 16 (16½, 17)" [40.5 (42, 43) cm] at seam line. End off.

Sew shoulder seams.

Front and Neck Bands

Note: To help pick up stitches evenly, divide fronts in 4 sections and mark with a different colored thread.

Row 1: With RS facing, using smaller hook, join yarn at bottom right-hand corner of Right Front, ch 1, work 59 (63, 67) sc evenly spaced across to top of neck, having 15 (16, 17) sts in each quarter section, work 3 sc in corner st, work 20 (22, 24) sc evenly spaced across neck edge to shoulder seam, work 32 (34, 36) sc evenly spaced across back of neck, work 20 (22, 24) sc evenly spaced across Left Front neck edge, work 3 sc in corner st, work 60 (64, 68) sc evenly space across Left Front edge, distributing them same as on Right Front, turn.

Row 2: Ch 1 (counts as first sc), sk first sc, 1 sc in each sc across, working 3 sc in each corner st, 1 sc in top of tch, turn.

Row 3 (buttonhole row): Ch 1 (counts as first sc), sk first sc, 1 sc in each sc across until 2 sts before center st of first corner, ch 2, sk next 2 sc (for buttonhole), work 3 sc in corner st, 1 sc in each sc across, 1 sc in top of tch, turn.

Row 4: Work same as Row 2, working 2 sc in ch-2 space of buttonhole, turn.

Row 5: Ch 1 (counts as first sc), sk first sc, sc in each sc to corner, 3 sc corner st, ch 3, (sc, ch 3, sc) in each sc across neck edge to corner at top of Left Front, 3 sc corner st, sc in each sc across. End off.

Finishing

Mark center top of Sleeve, pin sleeve in place, centering on shoulder, and ending by markers, sew sleeves in place. Sew underarm and side seams. Sew button on Left Front opposite buttonhole.

Blocking: Place on a padded surface, such as several towels. Spritz with water till garment is wet but not saturated. Pat into shape, pinning if necessary (be sure to use rustproof pins). Place a second towel on top, allow to dry.

shell stitch shoulder wrap

The lacy, open pattern of this shoulder wrap is created by a shell stitch, done in either knit or crochet. In crochet, a shell stitch is made by working five double crochets in the same stitch. To mimic this in knit, you wrap stitches in one row, drop them in the next, and purl groups of dropped stitches together. It's amazing how similar the two stitch patterns look. Also a-MAIZing is the flat ribbon yarn, made from 100-percent corn fiber. It makes a lightweight garment with lovely drape, and you can wash and dry it by machine.

Shell Stitch Shoulder Wrap
Knit

YARN

Medium-weight ribbon yarn

4 MEDIUM

Shown: *a-MAIZing* by SWTC, 100% corn fiber, 1.8 oz. (50 g)/142 yd. (128 m): berry #373, 7 skeins

NEEDLES

Size 7 (4.5 mm) or size to obtain correct gauge

STITCHES

Knit
Purl
Wrap/drop

GAUGE

3½ shells = 4" (10 cm)
Take time to check gauge.

NOTIONS/SUPPLIES

Tapestry needle

SIZE

16" x 56" (40.5 x 142 cm)

Wrap

Note: Row 3 begins and ends with half shell.

Pattern Stitch

Rows 1 and 2: Knit.

Row 3: Sl1, k2, (k1, yo, k1) in next st, *[wrap yarn twice, k1] 5 times, (k1, yo, k1, yo, k1) in next st; rep from * 11 times more, [wrap yarn twice, k1] 5 times, end (k1, yo, k1) in next st, k3.

Row 4: Sl1, k5, *holding yarn to front, slip 5 dropping extra wraps, then insert left-hand needle back into these 5 long sts and p5tog; k5; rep from * 12 times, ending last rep k6 instead of k5 (13 shells).

Rows 5 and 6: Knit.

Row 7: Sl1, k2 [wrapping yarn twice, k1] 3 times, *(k1, yo, k1, yo, k1) in next st, [wrapping yarn twice, k1] 5 times; rep from * 11 times more, end (k1, yo, k1, yo, k1) in next st, [wrap twice, k1] 3 times, k3.

Row 8: Sl1, k2, with yarn to front, slip 3, dropping extra wraps, insert left hand needle into these 3 sts and p3tog, *k5, with yarn front slip 5 dropping extra wraps, insert left hand needle into these 5 sts and p5tog; rep from * 11 times, end k5, yarn to front slip 3 dropping extra wraps, insert needle into these 3 sts and p3tog, k3—12 shells, half shell each side.

Rep Rows 1–8 for patt.

Cast on 85 sts. Work patt until 56" (142 cm) long, end with Row 1. Bind off in knit.

Finishing

To block, place on a towel, spritz lightly, and pat into shape.

Shell Stitch Shoulder Wrap crochet

YARN

Medium-weight ribbon yarn

Shown: *a-MAIZing* by SWTC, 100% corn fiber, 1.8 oz. (50 g)/142 yd. (128 m): berry #373, 8 skeins

HOOKS

Size G-6 (4 mm) or size to obtain correct gauge

STITCHES

Chain stitch
Single crochet
Double crochet

GAUGE

3½ shells = 4" (10 cm)
Take time to check gauge.

NOTIONS/SUPPLIES

Tapestry needle

SIZE

16" x 56" (40.5 x 142 cm)

Wrap

Note: Pattern is worked in the BL of sts throughout.

Ch 79.

Foundation row: Starting in 2nd ch from hook, work 1 sc in each ch across row, turn—78 sc.

Row 1: Ch 3 (counts as first dc), working in BL of sts, 2 dc in first sc, *sk next 2 sc, 1 sc next sc, sk next 2 sc, 5 dc in next sc; rep from * 11 times, sk next 2 sc, 1 sc next sc, sk 2 sc, 3 dc in top of tch, turn—12 shells, ½ shell each side.

Row 2: Ch 1 (counts as first sc), sk first st, working in BL of sts, *sk next 2 dc, 5 dc in next sc, sk next 2 dc, 1 sc in next dc (center of shell); rep from * 12 times more, ending with last sc in top of tch, turn—13 shells.

Row 3: Ch 3 (counts as first dc), working in BL of sts, 2 dc in first sc, *sk next 2 dc, 1 sc in next dc (center of shell), sk next 2 dc, 5 dc in next sc; rep from * 11 times, sk next 2 dc, 1 sc in next dc, sk next 2 dc, 3 dc in top of tch, turn—12 shells, ½ shell each side.

Rep Rows 2–3 until piece measures 56" (142 cm) from beg.

Last row: Ch 1 (counts as first sc), sk first sc, sc in BL of each st across, sc in top of tch. End off.

Finishing

To block, lay on a towel, spritz lightly and pat into shape.

Man's Button Vest

Multicolored yarn worked in a twisted rib-stitch pattern gives this man's vest lots of interesting texture. The similar ribbed look in both methods is not difficult to achieve—the knitted version incorporates a twisted stitch, the crochet version front post triple crochets. Because of the difference in the height and length of the crochet and knit stitches, the only way to design these patterns was to simply work them out individually. Once I established the gauge for each method, I planned the number of stitches and rows to obtain the proper measurements for each size.

Man's Button Vest

Knit

YARN

Medium-weight smooth yarn

Shown: *Park Avenue Printed* by Lily Chin Signature Collection, 60% merino wool, 40% alpaca, 1.8 oz. (50 g)/109 yd. (98 m), blue #127: 8 (9, 10, 11) skeins

NEEDLES

Size 6 (4 mm)
Size 9 (5.5 mm) or sizes to obtain correct gauge

STITCHES

Knit
Purl
Twist

GAUGE

18 sts = 4" (10 cm) on size 9 needles
Take time to check gauge.

NOTIONS/SUPPLIES

Tapestry needle
Five ⅞" (2 cm) buttons
Sewing needle and thread

SIZE

Small (Medium, Large, X-Large)
Finished chest: 40 (42, 44, 46)"
  [101.5 (106.5, 112, 117) cm]

Back

Note: To make a twisted stitch, skip one stitch, knit the next stitch, knit the skipped stitch, drop both stitches off needle.

With size 6 needles, cast on 96 (100, 104, 108) sts. K1, p1 in ribbing for 2½ (2½, 2½, 2½)" [6.5 (6.5, 6.5, 6.5) cm]. Change to size 9 needles and work as follows:

Row 1 (RS): P3 (5, 7, 9), *twist 2, p2, twist 2, p6; rep from * 6 times more, end twist 2, p2, twist 2, p3 (5, 7, 9).

Row 2: K3 (5, 7, 9), *p2, k2, p2, k6; rep from * 6 times more, end p2, k2, p2, k3 (5, 7, 9).

Rep Patt Rows 1 and 2 until 13½ (14, 14½, 15)" [34.5 (35.5, 37, 38) cm] from beg.

Shape Armhole

At beg of next 2 rows, bind off 6 sts. Dec 1 st each side every other row 6 times. Work even on rem 72 (76, 80, 84), keeping patt as established, until armhole measures 11½ (12, 12½, 13)" [29 (30.5, 32, 33) cm], end with a WS row.

Shape Shoulder

At beg of next 2 rows, bind off 21 (22, 23, 24) sts. Bind off rem 30 (32, 34, 36) sts.

Right Front

Note: The 6 border sts are worked the same throughout, V neck dec is made after the 6 border sts as follows: k6 border sts, k2tog.

With size 6 needles, cast on 54 (56, 58, 60) sts.

Row 1 (RS): K6, *p1, k1; rep from * across row.

Row 2: *P1, k1; rep from * to last 6 sts, p1, k5.

Rep last 2 rows for 2½ (2½, 2½, 2½)" [6.5 (6.5, 6.5, 6.5) cm], end with a WS row.

Change to size 9 needles and work patt as follows:

Row 1 (RS): K6, p3, *twist 2, p2, twist 2, p6; rep from * 2 times more, end twist 2, p2, twist 2, p3 (5, 7, 9).

Row 2: K3 (5, 7, 9), *p2, k2, p2, k6; rep from * 2 times more, p2, k2, p2, k3, p1, k5. Rep last 2 patt rows until 13½ (14, 14½, 15)" [34.5 (35.5, 37, 38) cm] from beg, end with an RS row.

Shape Armhole and V-Neck

At beg of next row (arm side), bind off 6 sts. Cont in patt as established, dec 1 st at arm side every other row 6 times; AT THE SAME TIME, dec 1 st neck edge and rep neck dec every 6th row 2 times more, then every 4th row 12 (13, 14, 15) times until 27 (28, 29, 30) sts rem. Work even until armhole measures 11½ (12, 12½, 13)" [29 (30.5, 32, 33) cm], end at arm side.

Shape Shoulder and Neck Tab

At beg of next row, bind off 21 (22, 23, 24) sts. Work even on rem 6 sts as established until tab measures 2½ (3, 3½, 4)" [6.5 (7.5, 9, 10) cm]. Bind off.

Left Front

Notes:

1. Before beginning left front, mark completed right front for 5 evenly spaced buttonholes, having the first one about ½" (1.3 cm) from bottom and the fifth one at start of V-neck shaping; use as a guide for placement of buttonholes on left front.

2. The 6 border sts are worked the same throughout, V neck dec is made before the 6 border sts as follows: work patt to last 8 sts, k2tog, k6 border sts.

With size 6 needles, cast on 54 (56, 58, 60) sts.

Row 1 (RS): *K1, p1; rep from * across row to last 6 sts, k6.

Row 2: K5, p1, *k1, p1; rep from * across row.

Rep last 2 rows for 2½ (2½, 2½, 2½)" [6.5 (6.5, 6.5, 6.5) cm], end with a WS row. Make first button

hole as follows (it takes 2 rows to complete buttonhole):

First Buttonhole Row (right side of work): Follow pattern as established to last 5 sts, k2, bind off next st, k last 2 sts.

Second Buttonhole Row: K2, cast on 1 st over the bound off st, k2, follow pattern as established to end of row.

Change to size 9 needles and work patt as follows:

Row 1 (RS): P3 (5, 7, 9), *twist 2, p2, twist 2, p6; rep from * 2 times more, twist 2, p2, twist 2, p3, k6.

Row 2: K5, p1, k3, *p2, k2, p2, k6; rep from * 2 times more, p2, k2, p2, k3 (5, 7, 9).

Rep last 2 patt rows until 13½, (14, 14½, 15)" [34.5 (35.5, 37, 38) cm] from beg, end with a WS row.

(continued)

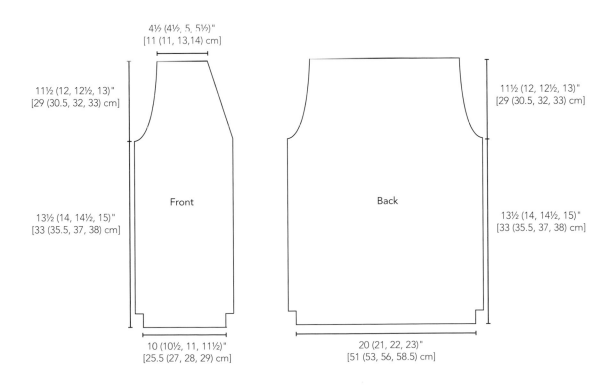

4½ (4½, 5, 5½)" [11 (11, 13,14) cm]

11½ (12, 12½, 13)" [29 (30.5, 32, 33) cm]

Front

13½ (14, 14½, 15)" [33 (35.5, 37, 38) cm]

10 (10½, 11, 11½)" [25.5 (27, 28, 29) cm]

11½ (12, 12½, 13)" [29 (30.5, 32, 33) cm]

Back

13½ (14, 14½, 15)" [33 (35.5, 37, 38) cm]

20 (21, 22, 23)" [51 (53, 56, 58.5) cm]

Man's Button Vest (continued)

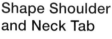

Shape Armhole and V-Neck

At the beg of the next row (from arm side), bind off 6 sts, cont in patt as established, dec 1 st at arm side every other row 6 times, AT THE SAME TIME dec 1 st at neck edge and rep the neck dec every 6th row two times more, then every 4th row 12 (13, 14, 15) times until 27 (28, 29, 30) sts rem. Work even until armhole measures 11½ (12, 12½, 13)" [29 (30.5, 32, 33) cm], end at arm side.

Shape Shoulder and Neck Tab

At beg of next row, bind off 21 (22, 23, 24) sts. Work even on rem 6 sts as established until tab measures 2½ (3, 3½, 4)" [6.5 (7.5, 9, 10) cm]. Bind off.

Finishing

Sew shoulder seams. Sew short ends of neck tabs tog, pin to back of neck, sew in place.

Armbands

With size 6 needle and RS facing, starting at underarm, pick up 70 (72, 74, 76) sts to shoulder seam, then pick up 70 (72, 74, 76) sts along other side—140 (144, 148, 152) sts. Work k1, p1 in ribbing for 1" (2.5 cm). Bind off in rib patt.

Sew side seams. Sew on buttons.

If blocking is needed, place vest on a towel, spritz lightly with water, pat into shape. Place another towel on top, allow to dry. Do not press with iron.

Man's Button Vest

crochet

YARN

Medium-weight smooth yarn

Shown: *Park Avenue Printed* by Lily Chin Signature Collection, 60% merino wool, 40% alpaca, 1.8 oz. (50 g)/109 yd. (98 m): blue #127, 9 (10, 11, 12) skeins

HOOKS

Size G-6 (4 mm)
Size I-9 (5.5 mm) or sizes to obtain correct gauge

STITCHES

Single crochet
Front post triple crochet

GAUGE

12 sts = 4" (10 cm) with I-9 hook
Take time to check gauge.

NOTIONS/SUPPLIES

Tapestry needle
Five ⅞" (2 cm) buttons
Sewing needle and thread

SIZE

Small (Medium, Large, X-Large)
Finished chest: 40 (42, 44, 46)"
[101.5 (106.5, 112, 117) cm]

Back

Notes:

1. Front post triple crochet (FPtr): Yarn over twice, insert hook from front to back to front again around the post of next st, yo, draw yarn through st, [yo, draw yarn through 2 loops on hook] 3 times

2. Sc2tog: Insert hook in next st, yo, draw yarn through st, insert hook in next st, yo, draw yarn through st, yo, draw yarn through 3 loops on hook.

Bottom ribbed band: With a smaller hook, ch 12 (12, 12, 12).

Foundation row: Starting in 2nd ch from hook, 1 sc in each ch across, turn—11 sc.

Row 1: Ch 1 (counts as first sc), sk the first sc, working in BL of sts, 1 sc in each of next 10 sc, 1 sc in top of tch—12 sts.

Rep Row 1 until 94 (96, 98, 100) rows [47, (48, 49, 50) ridges] have been worked. Do not end off. You will now be working along the row ends on the long edge of Band.

Row 1 (RS): Ch 1 (counts as a first sc), work 61 (63, 65, 67) sc evenly space across, turn—62 (64, 66, 68) sts.

Change to larger hook.

Row 2: Ch 1, skip first st, 1 sc in each st across, 1 sc in top of tch.

Row 3: Ch 1 (counts as a first sc), sk first sc, 1 sc in each of the next 4 (5, 6, 7) sc, *1 FPtr around the post of next sc 2 rows below, sk sc behind FPtr just made, 1 sc in next sc, 1 FPtr around the post of next sc 2 rows below, sk sc behind FPtr just made, 1 sc in each of the next 4 sc; rep from * 7 times more, 1 sc in each of last 1 (2, 3, 4) sts, turn   62 (64, 66, 68) sts.

Row 4: Ch 1 (counts as a sc), sk first sc, 1 sc in each st across row, turn.

Row 5: Ch 1 (counts as first sc), sk first sc, 1 sc in each of next 4 (5, 6, 7) sts , *1 FPtr around the post of next FPtr 2 rows below, sk sc behind FPtr just made, 1 sc next sc, 1 FPtr around the post of next FPtr 2 rows below, sk sc behind FPtr just made, 1 sc in each of the next 4 sc; rep from * 7 times more, 1 sc in each of last 1 (2, 3, 4) sts, turn.

Rep Rows 4—5 until piece measures 13½ (14, 14½, 15)" [34.5 (35.5, 37, 38) cm] from beg, ending with a WS row.

Man's Button Vest (continued)

Shape Armhole

Sl st over first 5 sts, ch 1, starting in next st, work in established patt across to within last 5 sts, turn, leaving remaining sts unworked.

Working in established patt, dec 1 st on each end of every other row 4 times, then work even on rem 44 (46, 48, 50) sts until armhole measures 11½ (12, 12½, 13)" [29 (30.5, 32, 33) cm]. End off.

Left Front

With smaller hook, work band same as back band until 48 (48, 50, 50) rows (24, 24, 25, 25 ridges) have been completed.

Row 1 (RS): Working across row-end sts of band, ch 1 (counts as first sc), work 30 (31, 32, 33) sc evenly spaced across long edge of band, turn—31 (32, 33, 34) sts.

Change to larger hook.

Row 2: Ch 1 (counts as sc), sk first st, 1 sc in each st across, 1 sc in top of tch.

Row 3: Ch 1 (counts as first sc), sk first sc, 1 sc in each of next 4 (5, 6, 7) sts, *1 FPtr around the post of next sc 2 rows below, sk sc behind FPtr just worked, 1 sc next st, 1 FPtr around the post of next sc 2 rows below, sk sc behind FPtr just worked**, 1 sc in each of next 4 sc; rep from * across ending last rep at **, 1 sc in next sc, 1 sc in top of tch, turn.

Row 4: Ch 1 (counts as first sc), sk first sc, 1 sc in each st across, 1 sc in top of tch, turn.

Row 5: Ch 1 (counts as first sc), sk first sc, 1 sc in each of next 4 (5, 6, 7) sts, *1 FPtr around the post of next FPtr, sk sc behind FPtr just worked, 1 sc next st, 1 FPtr around the post of next FPtr, sk sc behind FPtr just worked**, 1 sc in each of the next 4 sc; rep from * across, ending last rep at **, 1 sc in next sc, 1 sc in top of tch, turn.

Rep Rows 4–5 until piece measures 13½ (14, 14½, 15)" [34.5 (35.5, 37, 38) cm] from beg, ending with a WS row at armhole edge.

Shape Armhole and Neck

Sl st over first 5 sts, ch 1, starting in next st, work in established patt across, turn—26 (27, 28, 29) sts.

Work in established patt, dec 1 st at armhole side every other row 4 times AND AT THE SAME TIME, start neck shaping by dec 1 st at neck edge on 4th row, then dec 1 st on neck edge every 3rd row until 15 (16, 17, 18) sts rem. Work even until armhole measures 11½ (12, 12½, 13)" [29 (30.5, 32, 33) cm]. End off.

Right Front

Work same as Left Front through Row 2.

Change to larger hook.

Row 3 (RS): Ch 1 (counts as first sc), sk first sc, 1 sc in next sc, *1 FPtr around the post of next sc 2 rows below, sk sc behind FPtr just worked, 1 sc next st, 1 FPtr around the post of next sc 2 rows below, sk sc behind FPtr just worked, 1 sc in each of the next 4 sc, rep from * across, 1 sc in each of last 1 (2, 3, 4) sts, turn—31 (32, 33, 34) sts.

Row 4: Ch 1 (counts as first sc), sk first sc, 1 sc in each st across, 1 sc in top of tch, turn.

Row 5: Ch 1 (counts as first sc), sk first sc, 1 sc in next sc, *1 FPtr around the post of next FPtr 2 rows below, sk sc behind FPtr just worked, 1 sc next st, 1 FPtr around the post of next FPtr 2 rows below, sk sc behind FPtr just worked, 1 sc in each of the next 4 sc, rep from * across, 1 sc in each of last 1 (2, 3, 4) sts, turn.

Rep Rows 4–5 until piece measures 13½ (14, 14½, 15)" [34.5 (35.5, 37, 38) cm] from beg, ending with a WS row at front edge.

Shape Armhole and Neck

Work in established patt across to within last 5 sts, turn, leaving last 5 sts unworked.

Work in established patt, dec 1 st at armhole side every other row 4 times AND AT THE SAME TIME, start neck shaping, by dec 1 st at neck edge on 4th row, then dec 1 st on neck edge every 3rd row until 15 (16, 17, 18) sts rem. Work even until armhole measures 11½, (12, 12½, 13)" [29 (30.5, 32, 33) cm]. End off.

Finishing

Sew shoulder seams and side seams.

Button Band

Row 1: With RS facing, join yarn in bottom right corner of Right Front, ch 1 (counts as first sc), work 10 sc evenly spaced across band, work 25 (26, 27, 28) sc evenly spaced across Right Front to start of V neck shaping, work 35, (36, 37, 38) sc evenly spaced across to neck edge, work 21 (22, 23, 24) sc evenly spaced across Back neck edge, work 35 (36, 37, 38) sc evenly space down Left Front to start of V shaping, work 25 (26, 27, 28) sc evenly spaced across to bottom band, work 10 sc evenly spaced across band, turn—161 (166, 171, 176) sts.

Row 2: Ch 1 (counts as first sc), sk first st, 1 sc in each sc across, sc in top of tch, turn

Row 3 (buttonhole row): Ch 1 (counts as first sc), sk first st, 1 sc in each sc across to end of V shaping on left front, *ch 2, sk next 2 st, 1 sc in each of the next 6 sc; rep from * 3 times more, ch 2, sk next 2 sts, 1 sc in each rem st to end of row, turn.

Row 4: Ch 1 (counts as first sc), sk first st, 1 sc in each st across, working 2 sc in each ch-2 sp, turn.

Row 5: Ch 1 (counts as first sc), sk first sc, 1 sc in each sc across, sc in top of tch, turn. End off.

Sew on buttons.

If blocking is needed, lay vest on a towel, spritz lightly with water, pat into shape, place another towel on top, allow to dry. Do not press with iron.

Tweener cropped Jacket

The basket weave pattern used for this little cropped jacket looks really similar in knit and crochet. While swatching, I found that to get the same scale for both, I would have to use a double strand of yarn for knitting. As a result, I chose a very lightweight sock yarn and used it double-stranded for the knitted jacket and single-stranded for the crocheted one.

Tweener Cropped Jacket

Knit

YARN

Superfine yarn
Shown: *Aussi Sock Yarn* by Oasis
  Yarns, 90% superwash merino
  wool, 10% nylon, 3.5 oz.
  (100 g)/400 yd. (360 m):
  amethyst WS03, 4 (4, 5) skeins

NEEDLES

Size 5 (3.75 mm)
Size 7 (4.5 mm) or sizes to
  obtain correct gauge

STITCHES

Garter stitch
Basket weave

GAUGE

20 sts = 4" (10 cm) double-
  stranded on size 7 needles
  in basket weave patt
Take time to check gauge.

NOTIONS/SUPPLIES

Stitch holder
Tapestry needle
Eight ¾" (2 cm) decorative
  buttons
Sewing needle and thread
One ¾" (2 cm) plain button

SIZE

Girls' sizes 12 (14, 16)
Finished chest: 30½ (34, 36½)"
  [77.5 (86.5, 92.5) cm]

Back

Note: Yarn is used double-stranded throughout.

With size 5 needles, cast on 76 (84, 92) sts.

Work garter st (k every row) for 6 rows.

Change to size 7 needles and work patt as follows:

Rows 1, 3, 5: *K4, p4; rep from * 8 (9, 10) times more, end k4.

Rows 2, 4, 6: *P4, k4; rep from * 8 (9, 10) times more, end p4.

Rows 7, 9, 11: *P4, k4; rep from * 8 (9, 10) times more, end p4.

Rows 8, 10, 12: *K4, p4; rep from * 8 (9, 10) times more, end k4.

Rep the 12 patt rows until 4½ (5½, 6½)" [11.5 (14, 16.5) cm] from beg.

Shape Armhole

Being sure to keep patt as established, at beg of next 2 rows, bind off 4 (4, 4) sts. Dec 1 (1, 1) st each side every other row 4 times. Work even on rem 60 (68, 76) sts until armhole measures 6½ (7, 7½)" [16.5 (18, 19) cm].

Shape Shoulder

At beg of next 2 rows, bind off 18 (20, 22) sts. Place rem 24 (28, 32) sts on a holder to be worked later for neckband.

Left Front

With size 5 needles, cast on 50 (54, 58) sts.

Work garter st (k every row) for 6 rows.

Change to size 7 needles and work patt as follows:

Notes:
1. The 2 sts at front edge are always k2.

2. There is only 1 buttonhole top of Left Front.

Pattern Stitch for Size 12

Rows 1, 3, 5: *K4, p4, rep from * 5 times more, end k2.

Rows 2, 4, 6: K6, *p4, k4, rep from * 4 times more, end p4.

Rows 7, 9, 11: *P4, k4, rep from * 5 times more, end k2.

Rows 8, 10, 12: K2, *p4, k4, rep from * 5 times more.

Rep the 12 rows for patt.

Pattern Stitch for Size 14

Rows 1, 3, 5: *K4, p4, rep from * 5 times more, end k6.

Rows 2, 4, 6: K2, *p4, k4, rep from * 5 times more, end p4.

Rows 7, 9, 11: *P4, k4, rep from * 5 times more, end p4, k2.

Rows 8, 10, 12: *K6, * p4, k4, rep from * 5 times more.

Rep 12 rows for patt.

Pattern Stitch for Size 16

Rows 1, 3, 5: *P4, k4, rep from * 6 times more, end k2.

Rows 2, 4, 6: K2, *p4, k4, rep from * 6 times more.

Rows 7, 9, 11: *K4, p4, rep from * 6 times more, end k2.

Rows 8, 10, 12: K6, *p4, k4, rep from * 5, times more, end p4,

Rep the 12 rows for patt.

Work patt until piece measures 4 (5, 6)" [10 (12.5, 15) cm] from beg, end at arm side.

Shape Armhole

Being sure to keep patt as established, at beg of next row, bind off 4 (4, 4) sts. Dec 1 (1, 1) st arm side every other row 4 times. Work even on rem 42 (46, 50) sts until armhole measures 6 (6½, 7)" [15 (16.5, 18) cm], end at neck edge.

Buttonhole Row 1: Being sure to keep patt as established, k2, knit or purl next st, bind off 2 sts, cont patt to end of row.

Buttonhole Row 2: Work patt to bound-off buttonhole sts, using cable cast on method, cast on 2 sts to complete buttonhole, finish row.

Work 2 more rows, end at front edge.

*Note: For cable cast-on, *insert the right needle in the space behind the first stitch on the left needle, wrap the yarn over the needle and knit it as a stitch. Slip the stitch onto the left needle. Repeat from * for designated number of stitches.*

Shape Neck

At front edge, bind off 18 (20, 22) sts. Being sure to keep patt as est, dec 1 st neck edge every row 6 (6, 6) times. Work even until same as Back. Bind off rem 18 (20, 22) sts.

Right Front

Note: Before beginning Right Front, mark completed Left Front for four evenly spaced buttons, having first button 3" (7.5 cm) from bottom edge, and last button to match buttonhole on Left Front. Use this as a guide for placement of buttonholes on Right Front. All buttonholes will be made as on Left Front, working buttonholes in the 4th and 5th stitch in from front edge.

With size 5 needles, cast on 50 (54, 58) sts.

Work garter st (k every row) for 6 rows

Change to size 7 needles and work patt as follows:

Note: The 2 sts at front edge are always knit.

(continued)

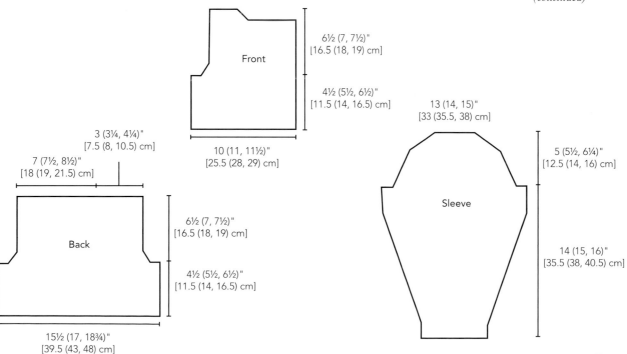

6½ (7, 7½)"
[16.5 (18, 19) cm]

Front

4½ (5½, 6½)"
[11.5 (14, 16.5) cm]

3 (3¼, 4¼)"
[7.5 (8, 10.5) cm]

7 (7½, 8½)"
[18 (19, 21.5) cm]

10 (11, 11½)"
[25.5 (28, 29) cm]

13 (14, 15)"
[33 (35.5, 38) cm]

5 (5½, 6¼)"
[12.5 (14, 16) cm]

Back

Sleeve

6½ (7, 7½)"
[16.5 (18, 19) cm]

4½ (5½, 6½)"
[11.5 (14, 16.5) cm]

14 (15, 16)"
[35.5 (38, 40.5) cm]

15½ (17, 18¾)"
[39.5 (43, 48) cm]

Pattern Stitch for Size 12

Rows 1, 3, 5: K2, *k4, p4; rep from * 5 times more.

Rows 2, 4, 6: *K4, p4; rep from * 5 times more, end k2.

Rows 7, 9, 11: K2, *p4, k4; rep from * 5 times more.

Rows 8, 10, 12: *P4, k4; rep from * 5 times more, end k2.

Rep the 12 rows for patt.

Pattern Stitch for Size 14

Rows 1, 3, 5: K2, *k4, p4; rep from * 5 times more, end k4.

Rows 2, 4, 6: *P4, k4; rep from * 5 times more, end k2.

Rows 7, 9, 11: K2, *p4, k4; rep from * 5 times more, end p4.

Rows 8, 10, 12: *K4, p4; rep from * 5 times more, end k6.

Rep 12 rows for patt.

Pattern Stitch for Size 16

Rows 1, 3, 5: K2, *k4, p4; rep from * 6 times more.

Rows 2, 4, 6: *K4, p4; rep from * 6 times more, end k2.

Rows 7, 9, 11: K2, *p4, k4, rep from * 6 times more.

Rows 8, 10, 12: *P4, k4; rep from * 6 times more, end k2.

Rep the 12 rows for patt.

Work patt until 4 (5, 6)" [10 (12.5, 15) cm] from beg, end at arm side.

Shape Armhole

Being sure to keep patt as established, at beg of next row, bind off 4 (4, 4) sts. Dec 1 (1, 1) st arm side every other row 4 times. Work even on rem 42 (46, 50) sts until armhole measures 6 (6½, 7)" [15 (16.5, 18) cm] and 2 rows past the last buttonhole, end at neck edge.

Shape Neck

At neck edge, bind off 18 (20, 22) sts. Dec 1 st neck edge every row 6 (6, 6) times. Work even until armhole measures same as Back. Bind off rem 18 (20, 22) sts.

Sleeves

Make 2.

With size 5 needles, cast on 44 (44, 44) sts.

Work garter st (k every row) for 6 rows.

Change to size 7 needles. Work patt as Back for 6 rows. Inc 1 st each side of next row, being sure to keep patt as established, then rep inc every 6th (6th, 6th) row until there are

68 (72, 76) sts. Work even in patt until sleeve measures 14 (14½, 15)" [35.5 (37, 38) cm] from beg.

Shape Cap

At beg of next 2 rows, bind off 4 (4, 4) sts. Dec 1 (1, 1) st each side every other row until 20 (20, 20) sts rem. Bind off.

Neckband

Sew shoulder seams. Using size 5 needles, right side facing you, starting on the 9th st of the bound-off sts of Front, pick up 23 (23, 23) sts along Right Front neck, k24 (28, 32) sts from Back neck holder, pick up 23 (23, 23) sts along Left Front neck, omitting last 8 sts of bound-off neck sts—70 (74, 78) sts. Work garter st for 1" (2.5 cm). Bind off in k.

Finishing

Fold Sleeve in half, mark center. Pin Sleeve in place, centering on shoulder seam; sew in sleeve, easing cap to fit. Sew underarm and side seams. Sew on buttons. Because of the textured patt, blocking is not recommended for this garment.

Tweener Cropped JacKet

crochet

YARN

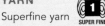

Superfine yarn
Shown: *Aussi Sock Yarn* by Oasis
Yarns, 90% superwash merino
wool, 10% nylon, 3.5 oz.
(100 g)/400 yd. (360 m):
amethyst WS03, 4 (4, 5) skeins

HOOKS

Size F-5 (3.75 mm)
Size G-6 (4 mm) or sizes to
obtain correct gauge

STITCHES

Chain stitch
Single crochet
Front post triple crochet
Back post triple crochet

GAUGE

20 sts = 4" (10 cm) in basket
weave pattern with larger hook
Take time to check gauge.

NOTIONS/SUPPLIES

Tapestry needle
Eight ¾" (2 cm) decorative
buttons
One ¾" (2 cm) plain button
Sewing needle and thread

SIZE

Girls' sizes 12 (14, 16)
Finished chest: 31 (34, 37½)"
[78.5 (86.5, 95.5) cm]

Back

Notes:

1. To decrease at underarms and neck edge: Ch 3, sk first st, work tr2tog in next 2 sts, work in patt across to within last 3 sts, tr2tog in next 2 sts, tr in top of tch.

2. Tr2tog (treble crochet decrease): Yo (twice), insert hook into st and draw up a lp, (yo and draw through 2 lps) twice, yo (twice), insert hook in next st and draw up a lp, yo, draw through 2 lps (twice), yo, draw through all lps on hook.

With smaller hook, ch 59 (67, 75). Foundation row: Starting in 2nd ch from hook, 1 sc in each ch across row, turn—58 (66, 74) sc.

Row 1: Ch 1 (counts as first sc), sk first sc, working in BL of sts, 1 sc in each of next 56 (64, 74) sts, 1 sc in top of tch, turn—58 (66, 74) sts.

Rows 2–4: Rep Row 1.

Row 5 for size 12: Ch 3 (counts as first dc), sk first sc, working in both loops of sts, *2 dc in next st (inc made), 1 dc in each of the next 2 sts; rep from * 17 times more, 2 dc in next st, 1 dc next st, 2 dc in top of tch, turn—78 dc.

Row 5 for size 14: Ch 3 (counts as first dc), 1 dc in same st (inc made),

working in both lps of sts, *1 dc in each of next 2 sc, 2 dc in next sc, 1 dc in each of next 3 sc, 2 dc next sc; rep from * 8 times more, 1 dc in next sc, 2 dc in top of tch, turn—86 dc.

Row 5 for size 16: Ch 3 (counts as first dc), sk first sc, working in both loops of sts, 1 dc in each of next 2 sc *2 dc in next sc, 1 dc in each of next 3 sc, 2 dc in next sc, 1 dc in each of next 2 sc; rep from * 9 times more, 1 dc in top of tch, turn—94 dc.

Change to larger hook, begin basket weave patt as follows:

Rows 1, 3, 6, and 8: Ch 3 (counts as first tr), sk first st, *work FPtr in next 4 sts, BPtr in next 4 sts; rep from * 8 (9, 10) times more, end with FPtr in next 4 sts, 1 tr in top of tch, turn—78 (86, 94) sts.

Rows 2, 4, 5, and 7: Ch 3 (counts as first tr), sk first st, *work BPtr in next 4 sts, FPtr in next 4 sts; rep from * 8 (9, 10) times more, end with BPtr in next 4 sts, 1 tr in top of tch, turn—78 (86, 94) sts.

Rep Rows 1–8 until piece measures 4½ (5½, 6½)" [11.5 (14, 16.5) cm].

Tweener
Cropped Jacket (continued)

Shape Armhole

Maintaining established patt, at the beg of the next row, sl st to 5th st, ch 3 (counts as first tr) work in established patt across to within last 5 sts, work 1 tr in next st, turn, leaving remaining sts unworked. Work in established patt, dec 1 st at each end of next 4 rows. Work even on rem 62 (70, 78) sts until armholes measure 6½ (7, 7½)" [16.5 (18, 19) cm] from beg. End off.

Left Front

Note: There is only 1 buttonhole at top of Left Front.

With smaller hook, ch 41 (45, 49). Foundation row: Starting in 2nd ch from hook, 1 sc in each ch across, turn—40 (44, 48) sc.

Row 1: Ch 1 (counts as first sc), sk first sc, working in BL of sts, 1 sc in each of next 38 (42, 46) sts, 1 sc in top of tch, turn—40 (44, 48) sts.

Rows 2–4: Rep Row 1.

Row 5 for size 12: Ch 3 (counts as first dc), sk first st, working in both loops of sts, 1 dc in each of next 5 sts, *2 dc in next st, 1 dc in each of next 2 sts; rep from * 9 times more, 1 dc in each of next 3 sts, 1 dc in top of tch, turn—50 dc.

Row 5 for size 14: Ch 3 (counts as first dc), sk first sc, working in both loops of sts, 1 dc in each of next 7 sc, *2 dc in next sc, 1 dc in each of the next 2 sc, rep from * 9 times more, 1 dc in each of next 5 sc, 1 dc in top of tch, turn—54 dc.

Row 5 for size 16: Ch 3 (counts as a dc, sk first sc, working in both loops of sts, 1 dc in each of next 8 sts, *2 dc in next sc, 1 dc in each of next 2 dc; rep from * 9 times more, 1 dc in each of next 8 sc, 1 dc in top of tch, turn—58 dc.

Change to larger hook, begin basket weave patt as follows:

Rows 1, 3, 6, and 8: Ch 3 (counts as first tr), sk first st, *work FPtr in next 4 sts, 4 BPtr in next 4 sts; rep from * 5 (5, 6) times more, work FPtr in next 0 (4, 0) sts, 1 tr in top of tch—50 (54, 58) sts.

Rows 2, 4, 5, and 7: Ch 3 (counts as first tr), sk first st, *work BPtr in next 4 sts, FPtr in next 4 sts; rep from * 5 (5, 6) times more, work BPtr in next 0 (4, 0) sts, 1 tr in top of tch, turn—50 (54, 58) sts.

Rep Rows 1–8 until piece measures 4½ (5½, 6½)" [11.5 (14, 16.5) cm] from beg, ending with a WS row at armhole edge.

Shape Armhole

Next row: Maintaining established patt, sl st to 5th st, ch 3 (counts as first tr), work in patt across, turn. Maintaining established patt, dec 1 st at armhole edge on each of next 4 rows. Work even on rem 42 (46, 50) sts until armhole measures 6 rows less than finished back, ending with a WS row.

Next row (buttonhole row): Work in patt across to within last 5 sts, work 1 post st in patt, ch 2, skip next 2 sts, work 1 post st in patt, 1 tr in top of tch, turn.

Next row: Ch 3 (counts as first tr), sk first st, work in established patt across, working 2 dc in ch-2 buttonhole space.

Shape Neck

Work in established patt on first 17 (19, 21) sts, turn, leaving rem 25 (27, 29) unworked. Then, maintaining patt, dec 1 st neck edge on each of next 3 rows, then work even on 14 (16, 18) sts until Front measures same as finished Back to shoulder. End off.

Right Front

Note: Before beginning Right Front, mark completed Left Front for four evenly spaced buttons, having first button 3" (7.5 cm) from bottom edge, and last button to match buttonhole on Left Front. Use this as a guide for placement of buttonholes on Right Front.

Work same as Left Front to armhole, except make a buttonhole on Right Front to correspond with each marker on Left Front, ending with a WS row on front edge.

Shape Armhole

Next row: Work in patt across to within last 5 sts, work 1 tr in next st, turn, leaving remaining sts unworked. Maintaining established patt, dec 1 st at armhole edge on each of next 4 rows. Work even on rem 42 (46, 50) sts until armhole measures 4 rows less than finished back, ending with a WS row.

Shape Neck

Sl st over 25 (27, 29) sts, ch 3 (counts as first tr), work in established patt across rem 17 (19, 21) sts, then dec 1 st at neck edge on each of next 3 rows, then work even on rem 14 (16, 18) until right front measures same as finished back to shoulder. End off.

Sleeves

Notes:

1. To make increases: Ch 3, do not sk first st, work tr in same st as tch, work in patt across, ending with 2 tr in top of tch. Form new patterns as stitches are increased.

2. To decrease at cap edges: Ch 3, sk first st, work tr2tog in next 2 sts, work in patt across to within last 3 sts, tr2tog in next 2 sts, tr in top of tch.

With smaller hook, ch 37. Foundation row: Starting in 2nd ch from hook, 1 sc in each st across, turn—36 sc.

Rows 2–6: Ch 1 (counts as first sc), working in BL of sts, 1 sc in each of next 34 sts, 1 sc in top of tch, turn—36 sts.

Row 7 (inc row): Ch 3 (counts as a dc) sk first sc, working in both loops of sts, 1 dc in each of next 3 sts, *2 dc in next st, 1 dc in each of next 2 sts; rep from * 9 times more, 1 dc in next st, 1 dc in top of tch, turn—46 dc.

Change to smaller hook, work even in established patt for 1 row, then maintaining patt, inc 1 st each end of next row and every 4th row thereafter until 66 (70, 74) sts are on work. Then, work even in patt until Sleeve measures 14 (15, 16)" [35.5 (38, 40.5) cm] from beg.

Shape Armhole

Sl st to 5th st, ch 3 (counts as first tr), work in established patt across to within last 5 sts, 1 tr in next st, turn, leaving remaining sts un-worked—58 (62, 66) sts.

Sleeve Cap

Cont in established patt, dec 1 st each end of every other row 7 (7, 8) times, then dec 1 st at each end of every row 5 (6, 7) times, then work even for 0 (1, 2) rows—34 (36, 36) sts. End off.

Finishing

Sew shoulder seams. Fold sleeve in half lengthwise. With center top of sleeve at shoulder seam, pin sleeve in place, sew in sleeve, easing cap to fit. Sew undercarm and side seams.

Neckband

Place a marker in 8th skipped st on left front neck edge.

Row 1: With RS facing, using smaller hook, skip first 8 sl sts on Right Front neck, join yarn in next st, ch 1 (counts as first sc), work 20 (22, 24) sc evenly spaced across Right Front neck edge to shoulder seam, work 28 (32, 36) sc evenly spaced across Back neck edge, work 21 (23, 25) sc evenly spaced across Left Front neck edge to marker, turn, leaving rem 8 sts unworked—70 (78, 86) sts.

Row 2: Ch 1 (counts as first sc), sk first st, working in BL of sts, sc in each st across, sc in top of tch, turn.

Rows 3–10: Rep Row 2. End off.

Front and Neck Edging

With smaller hook and RS facing, join yarn at bottom right corner of right front edge, ch 1, sc evenly across right front edge to top, work 3 sc in corner st, sc evenly across neck edge, and up side of neck-band, work 3 sc in corner st, sc in BL of each st across last row of neckband, work 3 sc in corner st, sc evenly across side of Neckband along top of Left Front neck edge, 3 sc in next corner st, sc evenly down Left front to bottom edge. End off.

Sew one button 2½" (6.5 cm) to the left of each buttonhole on right front. Sew plain button on WS of right front behind top button. With right front overlapping left front approx 2½" (6.5 cm), sew remaining buttons on left front to corrrespond with buttonholes. Blocking is not recommended for this garment.

baby sweater and Hat

For this adorable baby set, I chose two of my favorite stitches: trinity stitch in crochet and blackberry stitch in knitting. They provide a wonderful bubbly texture so perfect for a baby, and they look so remarkably similar that you really have to look closely to know which is which. Of course, using the same size needles and hook, the gauge is different. The knitted version requires more stitches to achieve the proper dimensions. Either version is lots of fun to make.

Baby Sweater and Hat

YARN

Lightweight smooth yarn **3 LIGHT**

Shown: *Beehive Baby Sport* by Patons, 70% acrylic, 30% nylon, 3.5 oz. (100 g)/359 yd. (323 m): delicate green #09230, 2 skeins for sweater, 1 skein for hat

NEEDLES

Size 4 (3.5 mm)
Size 5 (3.75 mm) or sizes to obtain correct gauge

STITCHES

Knit
Purl
Trinity stitch
Garter stitch

GAUGE

30½ sts = 4" (10 cm) in trinity st patt on size 5 needles
Take time to check gauge.

NOTIONS/SUPPLIES

Tapestry needle
Three ½" (1.3 cm) buttons
Sewing needle and thread

SIZE

12 mo (18 mo, 24 mo)
Finished chest: 22 (24, 26)"
  [56 (61, 66) cm]
Hat circumference: 16 (17, 18)"
  [40.5 (43, 45.5) cm]

Back

With size 5 needles, cast on 84 (92, 100) sts.

Knit 1 row.

Begin patt as follows:

Row 1 (RS): Purl.

Row 2: *(K1, p1, k1) all in next st, p3tog; rep from * across row.

Row 3: Purl.

Row 4: *P3tog, (k1, p1, k 1) all in next st; rep from * across row.

Rep Rows 1–4 until piece measures 6½ (7, 7½)" [16.5 (18, 19) cm].

Shape Armholes

At beg of next 2 rows, bind off 4 sts. Cont patt as established on rem 76 (84, 92) sts until armhole measures 5 (5½, 6)" [12.5 (14, 15) cm].

Shape Neck

At beg of next 2 rows, bind off 20 (22, 24) sts. Place rem 36 (40, 44) sts on holder to be worked later for neckband.

Left Front

With size 5 needles, cast on 49 (51, 53) sts. Work patt as for back, keeping 5 (3,5) sts at front edge in garter st (k every row), until piece measures same as back to armhole, end at arm side.

Shape Armhole

At beg of next row, bind off 4 sts. Cont patt as established on rem 45 (47, 49) sts until armhole measures 3 (3½, 4)" [7.5 (9, 10) cm], end at neck edge.

Shape Neck

At beg of next row, bind off 16 (16, 16) sts. Cont patt as established, dec 1 st neck edge every row 9 (9, 9) times. Work even in patt until armhole measures same as Back. Bind off rem 20 (22, 24) sts.

Right Front

Work same as Left Front to armhole, end at arm side.

Shape Armhole

At beg of next row, bind off 4 sts. Cont patt as established until armhole measures 2 (2¼, 2½)" [5 (5.5, 6.5) cm], end at neck edge.

First buttonhole: K1, yo, k2tog, finish row being sure to keep patt as established.

Work 3 more rows.

Rep last 4 rows once.

Third buttonhole: Rep Row 1 once.

Work even in patt as established until piece measures same as Left Front to neck shaping, end at neck edge.

Shape Neck

At beg of next row, bind off 16 (16, 16) sts. Cont patt as established, dec 1 st neck edge every row 9 (9, 9) times. Work even until piece measures same as Left Front to shoulder. Bind off rem 20 (22, 24) sts.

Sleeves

Make 2.

With size 4 needles, cast on 40 (42, 44) sts.

K 5 rows.

Next row: Inc 1 st in each st across row—80 (84, 88) sts. Change to size 5 needles. Work patt as Back until Sleeve measures 7½ (8, 8½)" [19 (20.5, 21.5) cm]. Bind off loosely.

Sew shoulder seams.

Neckband

With size 4 needles, starting ½" (1.3 cm) from front edge, pick up and k26 (28, 30) sts along Right Front neck edge, k36 (40, 44) from

Back neck holder, pick up and k26 (28, 30) sts along Left Front neck edge, end ½" (1.3 cm) in from front edge. Work garter st (k every row) for 1" (2.5 cm). Bind off.

Finishing

Fold Sleeve in half, mark center. Pin Sleeve in place centering on shoulder seam and ending at armhole bind off. Sew underarm and side seams. Sew buttons in place.

Blocking is not recommended for textured stitches.

(continued)

Baby Sweater and Hat (continued)

Hat

With size 4 needles, cast on 100 (104, 108) sts.

Work in garter st for 5 rows.

K next row, inc 24 sts evenly across row—124 (128, 132) sts.

Change to size 5 needles. Work patt until piece measures 5½ (6, 6½)" [14 (15, 16.5) cm] from beg.

Shape crown as follows:

K next row, dec 5 (9, 13) sts evenly across row—119 (119, 119) sts.

Next row: *K5, k2tog; rep from * across row—102 sts.

Next row: *K4, k2tog, rep from * across row—85 sts.

Next row: *K3, k2tog, rep from * across row—68 sts.

Next row: *K2, k2tog, rep from * across row—51 sts.

Next row: *K1, k2 tog; rep from * across row—34 sts.

Next row: K2tog all across row—17 sts.

Corkscrews

Make 3.

With double strand and size 5 needles, cast on 25 sts.

Row 1: (K1, pl, k1) in each st across row—75 sts.

Bind off, leaving enough yarn to sew to top of hat.

Stitch corkscrews to top of hat.

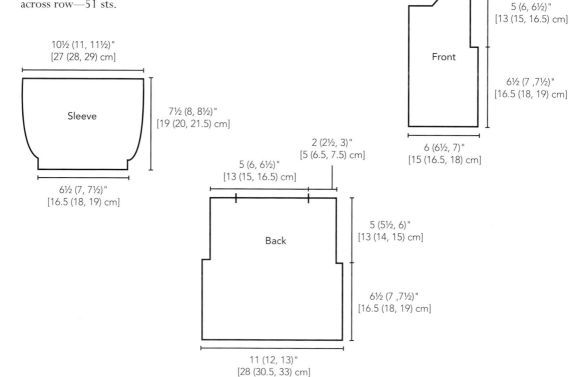

Baby Sweater and Hat

crochet

YARN

Lightweight smooth yarn

Shown: *Beehive Baby Sport* by Patons, 70% acrylic, 30% nylon, 3.5 oz. (100 g)/359 yd. (323 m): delicate green #09230, 2 skeins for sweater, 1 skein for hat

HOOKS

Size E-4 (3.5 mm)
Size F-5 (3.75 mm) or size to obtain correct gauge

STITCHES

Chain stitch
Single crochet
Blackberry stitch

GAUGE

18 sts = 4" (10 cm) in pattern stitch with larger hook
Take time to check gauge.

NOTIONS/SUPPLIES

Tapestry needle
Three ½" (1.3 cm) buttons
Sewing needle and thread

SIZE

12 mo (18 mo, 24 mo)
Finished chest: 22 (24, 26)" [56 (61, 66) cm]
Hat circumference: 16 (17, 18)" [40.5 (43, 45.5) cm]

Back

Notes:
1. Blackberry stitch (bbs): Draw up a lp in the next sc (yo, draw through last loop on hook) 3 times, forming a chain, keeping the ch 3 just made to front of work, yo, and draw through both loops on hook (blackberry stitch completed).

2. Sc2tog: Insert hook in next st, yo, draw yarn through st, insert hook in next st, yo, draw yarn through st, yo, draw yarn through 3 lps on hook.

With larger hook, ch 52 (56, 60).

Foundation row: Starting in 2nd ch from hook, 1 sc in each ch across, turn—51 (55, 59) sc.

Row 1 (RS): Ch 1 (counts as first sc), sk first sc, *work a blackberry stitch (bbs) in next sc, 1 sc in next sc; rep from * across, ending with 1 sc in top of tch, turn—51 (55, 59) sts.

Row 2: Ch 1 (counts as first sc), sk first st, 1 sc in each st across, 1 sc in top of tch, turn—51 (55, 59) sts.

Row 3: Ch 1 (counts as first sc), sk first sc, 1 sc next sc, *bbs in next sc, sc in next sc, rep from * across, ending with 1 sc in top of tch—51 (55, 59) sts.

Row 4: Rep Row 2.

Rep Rows 1–4 for pattern.

Work even in patt until Back measures 6½ (7, 7½)" [16.5 (18, 19) cm] from beg, ending with a WS row.

Shape Armhole

Sl st to 3rd st, work in established patt across to within last 2 sts, turn, leaving remaining sts unworked.

Work even in established patt on center 47 (51, 55) sts until armhole measures 5 (5½, 6)" [12.5 (14, 15) cm] from beg. End off.

Left Front

With larger hook, ch 28 (30, 32).

Foundation row: Starting in 2nd ch from hook, 1 sc in each ch across, turn—27 (29, 31) sc.

Work in bbs patt same as Back on 27 (29, 31) sts, rep Rows 1–4 for patt until piece measures 6½ (7, 7½)" [16.5 (18, 19) cm] from beg, ending with a WS row.

crochet

Shape Armhole

Sl st to 3rd st, work in established patt across, turn.

Work even in established patt on 25 (27, 29) sts until armhole measures 3 (3½, 4)" [7.5 (9, 10) cm] from beg, ending with an RS row at neck edge.

Shape Neck

Sl st over first 11 (12, 13) sts, ch 1, sk next st, work in established patt across rem 14 (15, 16) sts, turn.

Cont working in established patt, dec 1 st at neck edge on each of next 3 rows. Work even on rem 11 (12, 13) sts until armhole measures 5 (5½, 6)" [12.5 (14. 15) cm] from beg. End off.

Right Front

Work same as Left Front to armhole, ending with a WS row.

Shape Armhole

Work in established patt across first 25 (27, 29) sts, turn, leaving rem 2 sts unworked. Work even in established patt on 25 (27, 29) sts until armhole measures 3 (3½, 4)" [7.5 (9, 10) cm] from beg, ending with an RS row at armhole edge.

Shape Neck

Work in established patt across first 14 (15, 16) sts, turn, leaving rem 11 (12, 13) sts unworked.

Cont working in established patt, dec 1 st at neck edge on each of next 3 rows. Work even on rem 11 (12, 13) sts until armhole measures 5 (5½, 6)" [12.5 (14. 15) cm] from beg. End off.

Sleeves

Cuff: With smaller hook, ch 34 (36, 38).

Foundation Row: Starting in 2nd ch from hook, 1 sc in each ch across, turn—33 (35, 37) sc.

Row 1: Ch 1 (counts as first sc), sk first st, working BL of sts, 1 sc in each sc across, 1 sc in top of tch, turn—33 (35, 37) sts.

Rows 2–4: Rep Row 1.

Row 5: Ch 1 (counts as first sc), working in sc in both loops of sts, increase 14 sts evenly spaced across, turn—47 (49, 51) sts.

With smaller hook, work even in bbs patt same as Back until Sleeve measures 1" (2.5 cm) from top of Cuff. Change to larger hook, and cont working in established patt until Sleeve measures 7 (7½, 8)" [18 (19, 20.5) cm] from beg. End off.

Finishing

With RS of pieces facing each other, pin shoulder seams, then sew shoulder seams. Fold Sleeves in half lengthwise, with center top of Sleeve at shoulder seam, pin then sew Sleeves into armhole. Sew underarm and side seams.

Neckband

Note: Neckband starts and finishes ½" (1.3 cm) in from edges to allow for overlap when buttoned.

Row 1: With smaller hook and RS facing, and starting ½" (1.3 cm) to the left of Right Front edge, join yarn in next st on neck edge, ch 1 (counts as first sc), work 17 (18, 19) sc evenly spaced across Right

Front neck shaping to shoulder seam, work 30 (32, 34) sc across Back neck edge, work 18 (19, 20) sc evenly spaced across Left Front neck shaping, stopping ½" (1.3 cm) from Left Front edge, turn—66 (70, 74) sts.

Rows 2–5: Ch 1 (counts as first sc), sk first st, working in BL of sts, sc in each st across, sc in top of tch, turn. End off.

Starting just below neck edge on Left Front, sew buttons ¾" (2 cm) apart down left front edge. No need to make buttonholes, use open spaces bet sts as buttonholes.

Blocking is not recommended for textured stitches. If some blocking is required, spritz lightly with water, pat gently into place with fingers, allow to dry flat.

Hat

With smaller hook, ch 74 (78, 82).

Foundation row: Starting in 2nd ch from hook, 1 sc in each ch across, turn—73 (77, 81) sc.

Work in bbs patt same as Back on 73 (77, 81) sts, rep Rows 1–4 for patt until piece measures 6 (6½, 7)" [15 (16.5, 18) cm] from beg, ending with a WS row.

Shape crown as follows:

Row 1: Ch 1 (counts as first sc), sk first st, 1 sc in each st across, 1 sc in top of tch, turn—73 (77, 81) sts.

Row 2: Ch 1 (counts as first sc), sk first st, working in sc in BL of sts, dec 3 (7, 11) sts evenly spaced across, turn—70 sts.

Row 3: Ch 1 (counts as first sc), sk first st, working in sc in BL of sts, sc in each of next 4 sts, sc2tog in next 2 sts, *1 sc in each of the next 5 sc, sc2tog in next 2 sts; rep from * across, turn—60 sts.

Row 4: Ch 1 (counts as first sc), sk first st, working in sc in BL of sts, sc in each of next 3 sts, sc2tog in next 2 sts, *1 sc in each of the next 4 sc, sc2tog in next 2 sts; rep from * across, turn—50 sts.

Row 5: Ch 1 (counts as first sc), sk first st, working in sc in BL of sts, sc in each of next 2 sts, sc2tog in next 2 sts, *1 sc in each of the next 3 sc, sc2tog in next 2 sts; rep from * across, turn—40 sts.

Row 6: Ch 1 (counts as first sc), sk first st, working in sc in BL of sts, sc in next st, sc2tog in next 2 sts, *1 sc in each of the next 2 sc, sc2tog in next 2 sts; rep from * across, turn—30 sts.

Row 7: Ch 1 (counts as first sc), sk first st, sc2tog in next 2 sts, *1 sc in next st, sc2tog in next 2 sts; rep from * across, turn—20 sts.

Row 8: Ch 1 (counts as first sc), sk first st, *sc2tog in next 2 sts; rep from * across, ending with 1 sc in top of tch, turn—11 sts. End off, leaving an 18" (45.5 cm) sewing

length. Thread this end on a tapestry needle, gather sts along last row and draw up. Draw through again and knot, then sew back seam.

Corkscrews
Make 3.

With larger hook, using yarn double-stranded, ch 21. Starting in 2nd ch from hook, work 3 sc in each ch across. End off, leaving sewing length. Sew to top of hat.

entrelac Hat

You can knit or crochet the entrelac stitch pattern; both are a little challenging but well worth learning. In the knitted version, you work alternately from wrong and right sides. In the crocheted version, you always work from the right side. For both, you must end a color and start a new color, but don't carry yarn along the sides. Getting the right gauge is really important when you are making a hat, so choose the same yarn—or same weight of yarn—and make sure to test first. After all, I tested for hours to determine the needle sizes and number of stitches needed to make these nearly identical hats in both knit and crochet.

Entrelac Hat  knit

YARN

Medium-weight smooth yarn

Shown: *Baby Alpaca DK* by Plymouth Yarn, 100% baby alpaca, 1.8 oz. (50 g)/125 yd. (113 m): dark tan #208 (A), 2 skeins; light tan #207 (B), 1 skein; off-white #100 (C), 1 skein

NEEDLES

Size 5 (3.75 mm)
Size 7 (4.5 mm) or sizes to obtain correct gauge

STITCHES

Stockinette stitch

GAUGE

18 sts = 4" (10 cm) in stockinette st on size 7 needles
Take time to check gauge.

NOTIONS/SUPPLIES

Tapestry needle

SIZE

22" (56 cm) circumference unstretched

Hat

Notes:

1. Hat can be made with two colors using two skeins of A and one skein of B or C.

2. Yarn has to be ended and new color restarted after each entrelac row.

3. Entrelac is a series of little rectangles and half rectangles (called triangles from now on) of knitting attached to each other by both picking up stitches and knitting stitches together with ones from the previous tier. Every other tier is composed of nine full rectangles. The alternate rows are one triangle on each side and eight full rectangles in the center. Each triangle or rectangle is twenty rows. When finished, it almost looks like the tiers of blocks are woven.

4. Each rectangle (or triangle) is worked on ten stitches, using the short row method to create each section. When it says "turn," turn your work around completely and head back the way you came. You will notice p2tog at the end of many of the rows. This is where you are attaching the side of the rectangle that you are making to the top of the rectangle (or triangle) from the tier below. You purl together one stitch from the needle with one stitch from the side of the adjacent rectangle. This is explained in the directions only the first time it occurs.

5. Try not to stop in the middle of a tier. If you must stop, make a note of what direction you were going when you stopped.

Band

With size 5 needles and A, cast on 106 sts. K1, p1 in ribbing for 6" (15 cm).

K 1 row, dec 26 sts evenly spaced across row—80 sts.

Purl 1 row. End off A, join B. Change to size 7 needles, work entrelac patt as follows:

Base Tier (RS)

The base tier is made up of eight triangles. First triangle; *K2 turn, p2 turn, k3 turn, p3 turn, k4 turn, p4 turn, k5 turn, p5 turn, k6 turn, p6 turn, k7 turn, p7 turn, k8 turn, p8 turn, k9 turn, p9 turn, k10, do not turn (first half rectangle completed). Rep from * 7 times more—8 triangles in all. End B. Turn work to wrong side.
Note: Process photos do not show the entire tier.

Tier 2 (WS)

Join A. Tier 2 is made up of full rectangles, with a triangle each side.

Step 2A, first triangle: Begin by purling and knitting into the first st (inc made), purl the next 2 sts tog, tog (1 st from needle with 1 st from side of adjacent rectangle), turn the work, and k3, purl and knit into the first st (inc made) p1, p2tog, turn, k4. Cont in this manner, increasing 1 st in the first st, and having 1 more purl st before the p2tog, until there are 10 sts on right-hand needle. Do not turn after the last p2tog.

Step 2B, full rectangle: Leaving the 10 sts on the right-hand needle, begin to work a full rectangle on the wrong side as follows: inserting the needle from back to front, pick up and p10 sts along the side edge of the first triangle from the tier below. Slip the last st picked up back to the left-hand needle and purl it together with the first st of the second triangle, turn, *k10, turn, p9, p2tog (1 st from the next triangle) rep from * until all 10 sts from the triangle have been worked. The rectangle is now complete and joined to the second side of the triangle.

Rep Step 2B until all the rectangles are formed across row. You will have one triangle at beg and seven rectangles.

Step 2C, ending triangle: Pick up and p9 sts from unworked side of last triangle, turn, k9. Turn, p7, p2tog, turn, k8. Cont in this manner, purling 2 tog at the end of every wrong-side row until 1 st rem, turn—seven rectangles, one triangle each side. End A, join C.

(continued)

Entrelac Hat (continued)

Tier 3 (RS)

Tier 3 is made up of nine whole rectangles.

Step 3A: Counting the 1 st left on the right-hand needle, pick up and k9 sts along first triangle, k first st from full rectangle and sl last picked up st over it.

Step 3B: *Turn, p10, turn, k9, sl1 st, k1 st from rectangle and psso. Rep from * until all 10 sts from the rectangle have been worked and are on right-hand needle, pick up and k10 sts along the side edge of next rectangle.

Rep Step 3B until eight rectangles are completed. End C, join A.

Tier 4 (WS)

Rep Tier 2 with A. End A, join B.

Tier 5 (RS)

Rep Tier 3 with B. End B, join A.

Top Tier (WS)

Notes:

1. Closing triangles are worked across top to complete the rectangle.

2. Strip begins and ends with half triangles.

Beg half triangle as follows:

With WS facing you and col B, p and k into first st (inc made), p2tog. Turn, k3. Turn, p and k into first st (inc made), p1, p2tog. Turn, k4. Turn, p and k into first st, p2, p2tog. Turn, k5. Turn, p and k into first st, p3, p2tog. Turn, k6. Turn, p2tog, p3, p2tog. Turn, k5. Turn, p2tog, p2, p2tog. Turn, k4. Turn, p2tog, p1, p2tog. Turn, k3. Turn, p2tog, p2tog. Turn, k2tog, do not turn.

Beg first full triangle as follows:

*Pick up 9 sts down side of next rectangle, sl last st picked up to left-hand needle and p this st tog with first st on left-hand needle, turn, k10. Turn, p2tog, p7, p2tog. Turn, k9. Turn, p2tog, p6, p2tog. Turn, k8. Turn, p2tog, p5, p2tog. Turn, k7. Turn, p2tog, p4, p2tog. Turn, k6. Turn, p2tog, p3, p2tog. Turn, k5. Turn, p2tog, p2, p2tog. Turn, k4. Turn, p2tog, p1, p2tog. Turn, k3. Turn, p2tog, p2tog. Turn, k2. Turn, p2tog. Repeat from * 7 times more.

End half triangle as follows:.

Pick up 9 sts along end of last rectangle, turn, k10. Turn, p2tog, p8. Turn, k9. Turn, p2tog, p7. Turn, k8. Turn, p2tog, p4, p2 tog. Turn, k6. Turn, p2tog, p2, p2tog. Turn, k2tog, k2 tog. Turn, p2tog, end off, leaving a 24" (61 cm) length of yarn for sewing.

Finishing

Thread the 24" (61 cm) length of yarn onto a tapestry needle, gather the points of the ending triangles and pull tightly together. Do this at least 3 times to form the top of hat. (Hint: A Cibi needle with the bent point is very helpful in sewing the top of hat.) Sew the back seam.

Blocking is not recommended for this textured stitch.

Entrelac Hat
crochet

YARN

Medium-weight smooth yarn

Shown: *Baby Alpaca DK* by Plymouth, 100% baby alpaca, 1.8 oz. (50 g)/125 yd. (114 m): dark tan #208 (A), 2 skeins; light tan #207 (B), 1 skein; off-white #100 (C), 1 skein

HOOKS

Size F-5 (3.75 mm) and Size H-8 (5 mm) or sizes to obtain correct gauge

STITCHES

Chain stitch
Single crochet
Slip stitch
Tunisian

GAUGE

4 sts = 1" (2.5 cm) with larger hook in Tunisian simple stitch.
16 sts = 4" (10 cm) with smaller hook in sc in BL only Band pattern.
Take time to check gauge.

NOTIONS/SUPPLIES

Tapestry needle

SIZE

22" (56 cm) circumference unstretched

Hat

Notes: Entrelac crochet uses Tunisian method, with a standard crochet hook, as there are never more than ten stitches on the hook at any time (see directions for Tunisian stitches on page 127). This hat is worked by forming color strips comprised of a series of rectangles and triangles turned on their points. You are always working from the right side, never turning your work. When one strip is completed, end off that color, join new color at beginning of row and start again. In addition to the rectangles every other color strip will begin with a triangle (this evens out the ends). Each rectangle or triangle in the strip consists of ten rows.

Ribbed Band (worked vertically to create ribbing): Using size F-5 hook, with A, ch 27.

Foundation row: Starting in 2nd ch from hook, working in BL only, 1 sc in each ch across, turn—26 sc.

Row 1: Ch 1, sk first st, working in BL only, 1 sc in each of the next 25 sc, 1 sc in top of tch, turn.

Rep Row 1 until band measures 22" (56 cm) from beg. End off. Set band aside to be sewn to body of hat later.

Body of hat: For Hat work entrelac pattern, alternating strip colors A, C, A, B. Work top strip with A and bottom strip with B.

First Color Strip

This strip begins and ends with a triangle. With A, ch 133 loosely.

First Triangle:

Row 1: Draw up a lp in 2nd ch from hook (2 lps on hook), yo, draw through both lps on hook.

Row 2: Insert hook under first vertical bar and pick up a lp, then draw up a lp in next ch of foundation ch (3 lps on hook), (yo, draw through 2 lps on hook) twice (1 lp left on hook and counts as first st of next row).

Row 3: Insert hook BETWEEN first 2 bars and pick up a lp (inc made), draw up a lp from under next bar (of same st), draw up a lp in next ch of foundation ch (4 lps on hook), (yo, draw through 2 lps on hook) 3 times (1 lp left on hook).

Row 4: Insert hook between first 2 bars and pick up a lp (inc made), draw up a lp from under next bar (of same st), draw up a lp under bar of each st across, draw up a lp in next ch (5 lps on hook), *yo, draw through 2 lps on hook; rep from * until 1 lp remains on hook.

Rows 5–9: Rep Row 4—10 lps on first half of Row 9.

Row 10: Insert hook under next bar, draw yarn through bar and lp on hook (sl st worked), sl st under each bar across, sl st in same ch lp at base of last st of Row 9. DO NOT END OFF—continue making next rectangle as follows:

Rectangle 1:
Row 1 (Still on first color strip): Draw up a lp in each of next 9 ch (10 lps on hook), [yo and draw through 2 lps on hook] 9 times (1 lp left on hook and counts as first st of next row).

Row 2: Insert hook under the next bar, draw yarn through (2 lps on hook) draw up a lp in each of next 7 bars, sk last st of row, draw up a lp in next ch of foundation ch (10 lps on hook), work off lps as Row 1 of rectangle.

Rows 3–10: Rep Row 2.

Row 11: Sl st in each bar across, sl st same ch at base of last st of Row 10.

Rectangle 2:
(Still on first color strip): Draw up a lp in each of next 9 ch (10 lps on hook), work off as before, complete same as Rectangle 1.

Cont making rectangles in this way until six rectangles are complete— 9 ch sts remain on foundation ch.

Ending Triangle:
Row 1: Draw up a lp in each of the next 9 ch sts (10 lps on hook), [yo and draw through 2 lps] 9 times (1 lp left on hook and counts as first st of next row).

Row 2: Draw up a lp in each of the next 8 bars, sk last st (9 lps on hook), [yo and draw through 2 lps] 8 times (1 lp left on hook and counts as first st of next row).

Rows 3–9: Cont in this manner, always having 1 less lp each row, until 1 st remains in last row.

Row 10: Sl st under next bar. End off. This completes the first color strip—six rectangles with a triangle at each end. End off A. (Samples show only partial rows.)

(continued)

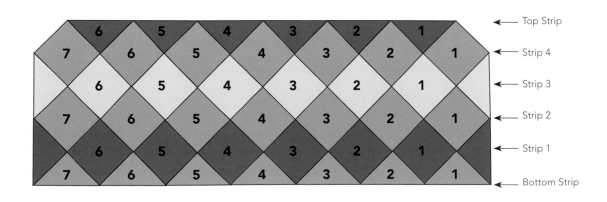

Entrelac Hat (continued)

Second Color Strip

This color strip begins and ends with a rectangle—seven rectangles total. Each rectangle has 10 rows.

Rectangle 1:

Row 1: With RS facing, join C in first sl st in Row 10 of first triangle on Strip 1, starting in same st, draw up 1 lp in each of next 8 sl sts, sk next sl st, pick up a lp in end of first row of first rectangle on Strip 1 (10 lps on hook), work off lps as before.

Row 2: Draw up a lp in each of next 8 bars, sk last st of row, draw up a lp in next row-end st on adjacent rectangle in Strip 1 (10 lps on hook), work off lps as before.

Rows 3–10: Rep Row 2.

Row 11: Sl st in each bar across, sl st in same row-end st at base of last st of Row 10.

Rectangle 2:

Row 1: Draw up a lp in each of next 8 sl sts, sk next sl st, pick up a lp in end of first row of first rectangle on Strip 1 (10 lps on hook), work off lps as before.

Complete same as Rectangle 1.

Rep Rectangle 2 five more times, ending at top of ending triangle in Strip 1—seven rectangles made.

Third Color Strip

With A, ch 2.

Row 1: With RS facing, with A, draw up a lp in 2nd ch from hook, pick up a lp in end of first row of first rectangle on Strip 2 (3 lps on hook), work off lps as before.

Work same as Triangle 1 on Strip 1, except at the end of each row, pick up a lp in row-end st on adjacent rectangle instead of in foundation ch. Then work a total of six rectangles same manner as on Strip 2. Then work ending triangle same as on Strip 1, working first row across top of last rectangle instead of in foundation ch.

Fourth Color Strip

With B work same as second color strip across top of third color strip.

Top Color Strip (Closing Triangles)

Notes:
1. Closing triangles are worked across top and bottom to complete the rectangle.

2. Top row begins and ends with half-size triangles. Work first half-size triangle as follows:

Row 1: With A, ch 2, draw up lp in first ch from hook and draw up a lp in side of first row of first rectangle of strip 4 (3 lps on hook), [yo, draw through 2 lps] 2 times. Insert hook bet first 2 bars and draw up lp (inc made), draw up lp from under next bar and next ch, (4 lps on hook, [yo, draw through 2 lps] 3 times (1 lp left on hook). Cont in this manner, having 1 st more each row, until you have 7 lps on hook. Work off as before.

Next row: Skip first 2 bars (dec made) draw up lp in each of the next 4 bars, draw up lp next ch (5 lps on hook). Work off as before.

Next row: Skip first 2 bars (dec made) draw up lp in each of the next 3 bars, draw up next ch (4 lps on hook). Work off as before.

Cont in this manner to dec beg of every row till 1 lp rems, sl st in last ch.

First full triangle:

Row 1: Draw up 8 lps along bound off edge of next rectangle, plus 1 lp in end of first row of second rectangle (10 lps on hook), work off as before.

Under First full triangle:

Row 2: Skip first 2 bars (skipping 2 bars only dec one st, as lp on hook counts as first bar), draw up lp in next 7 bars and 1 lp in end of second row of next rectangle (9 lps on hook), work off as before.

Row 3: Skip first 2 bars, draw up lp in next 6 bars and 1 lp in end of third row of next rectangle (8 lps on hook), work off as before.

Row 4: Skip first 2 bars, draw up lp in next 5 bars and 1 lp in end of fourth row of next rectangle (7 loops on hook), work off as before.

Row 5: Skip first 2 bars, draw up lp in next 4 bars and 1 lp in end of fifth row of next rectangle (6 loops on hook), work off as before.

Cont in this manner, always have 1 less lp on hook till 1 lp rems, sl st into last side st.

Repeat to fill in all full triangles.

Work last half-size triangle as follows:

Row 1: Draw up a lp in each of next 9 ch (10 lps on hook), work off as before.

Row 2: Sk first 2 bars (by skipping first 2 bars you are dec 1 st, as the lp on hook counts for the first bar as usual), draw up a lp in each of next 7 bars, sk last bar, work off as before.

Rows 3 and 4 : Cont in this manner, always having 2 less lps each row, until 2 lps on hook, draw 2 tog, end off.

Bottom Color Strip (Closing Triangles)

With B, work 7 full triangles across bottom, working in opposite side of foundation row.

Finishing

Pin Ribbed Band to the closing triangles on bottom color strip and sew into place.

Thread a 30" (76 cm) length of A onto a tapestry needle, weave through sts across top edge of top color strip, gather top of Hat, pull to close hole, rep gathering at least 2 times more to anchor securely, then sew back seam.

Fold Ribbed Band triple thickness.

Blocking is not recommended for this hat to preserve stitch texture.

Dapper Dog Coat

Pampered pooches need stylish jackets to keep them warm on cold-weather walks. These jackets are made with dense stitches for warmth with stripes of puff stitches for interest. Both versions have enough stretch to allow them to fit a variety of small, medium, or large dogs. Large snaps, accented with buttons, close the front and hold the underbelly strap in place.

Dapper Dog Coat

K knit

YARN

Medium-weight smooth yarn

Shown: *Wool-Ease* by Lion Brand, 80% acrylic, 20% wool, 3 oz. (85 g)/197 yd. (177 m): blue heather #107, 1 (2, 2) skeins

NEEDLES

Size 9 (5.5 mm) or size to obtain correct gauge

STITCHES

Knit
Purl
Popcorn
Garter

GAUGE

17 sts = 4" (10 cm)
Take time to check gauge.

NOTIONS/SUPPLIES

Tapestry needle
Stitch markers
Four ½" (1.3 cm) buttons
Four large snaps
Sewing needle and thread

SIZE

Small (Medium, Large)
Length (from base of neck to tail):
11½ (13½, 15½)" [29 (34.5, 39.5) cm]
Width: 11½ (13½, 15½)"
[29 (34.5, 39.5) cm]

Dog Coat

Bottom border:

Cast on 41 (49, 57) sts.

Rows 1, 3, 5, 7: Knit.

Rows 2, 4, 6, 8: K1, inc 1 st in the next st, k to last 2 sts , inc 1 st in next st, k last st—49 (57, 65) sts.

Beg patt:

Note: Slip markers as you come to them each row.

Row 1: K4, place marker, k to last 4 sts, place marker, k4.
Row 2: Knit.

Row 3: K4, *k1, sl1, rep from * to last 5 sts, k1, k4.

Row 4: K5, *yf (yarn in front), sl1, yb (yarn in back), k1, rep from * to last 4 sts, k4.

Rows 5 and 6: Knit.

Row 7: K4, *sl1, k1, rep from * to last 5, sl1, k4.

Row 8: K4, *yf, sl1, yb, k1, rep from * until last 5 sts, yf, sl1, yb, k4.

Rows 9–24: Rep Rows 1–8 two times more.

Row 25 (popcorn row): K5, *k in front, back, front of the next st, turn, p3, turn, sl1, k2tog, psso, k1, rep from * 19 (23, 27) times, end k4—20 (24, 28) popcorns.

Row 26: Knit.

Rep Patt Rows 1–26 until 11½ (13½, 15½)" [29 (34.5, 39.5) cm] from beg.

Shape Right Neck

Being sure to keep patt as established, work across 16 (19, 22) sts, place rem 33 (38, 43) sts on holder to be worked later. Cont in patt on center 8 (11, 14) sts, keeping 4 sts each side in garter st, for 3½ (4, 4½)" [9 (10, 11.5) cm]. Work 1" (2.5 cm) in garter st. Bind off.

Shape Left Neck

Place sts from holder onto needle, join yarn by right side, bind off center 17 (19, 21) sts, work rem 16 (19, 22) sts. Work on 16 (19, 22) sts as for right neck shaping. Bind off.

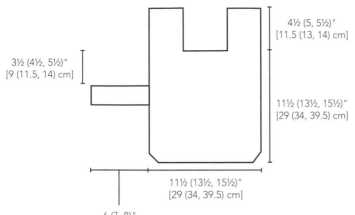

4½ (5, 5½)"
[11.5 (13, 14) cm]

3½ (4½, 5½)"
[9 (11.5, 14) cm]

11½ (13½, 15½)"
[29 (34, 39.5) cm]

11½ (13½, 15½)"
[29 (34, 39.5) cm]

6 (7, 8)"
[15 (18, 20) cm]

Under Belt

Starting at 3½ (4½, 5½)" [9 (11.5, 14) cm] from neck shaping, on left side of coat, right side facing you, pick up 10 (14, 18) sts. Work in garter st for 6 (7, 8)" [15 (18, 20.5) cm]. Bind off.

Finishing

Sew snaps on under belt and neck tabs; sew buttons over snaps.

Dapper Dog Coat

crochet C

YARN

Medium-weight smooth yarn **4** MEDIUM

Shown: *Wool-Ease* by Lion Brand, 80% acrylic, 20% wool, 3 oz. (85 g)/197 yd. (177 m) blue heather #107, 1 (2, 2) skeins

HOOKS

Size H-8 (5 mm) or size to obtain correct gauge.

STITCHES

Chain stitch
Single crochet
Triple crochet

GAUGE

13 sts and 15 rows = 4" (10 cm)
Take time to check gauge.

NOTIONS/SUPPLIES

Tapestry needle
Four ½" (1.3 cm) buttons
Four large snaps
Sewing needle and thread

SIZE

Small (Medium, Large)
Length (from base of neck to tail): 11½ (13½, 15½)" [29 (34.5, 39.5) cm]
Width: 11½ (13½, 15½)" [29 (34.5, 39.5) cm]

Dog Coat

Ch 32 (38, 44).

Foundation row: Starting in 2nd ch from hook, 1 sc in each ch across, turn—31, (37, 43) sc.

Row 1 (RS): Ch 1 (counts as first sc), sk first sc, working in BL of sts, 2 sc in the next st (inc made), 1 sc in each st across to within last 3 sc, 2 sc in each of next 2 sc (inc made), 1 sc in top of tch, turn—33 (39, 45) sts.

Rows 2–4: Rep Row 1—39 (45, 51) sc at end of last row.

Row 5: Ch 1 (counts as sc), sk first sc, sc in BL of next 3 sc, sc in both loops of next 32 (38, 44) sts, sc in BL on next 3 sts, sc in top of tch, turn—39 (45, 51) sts.

Rows 6–15: Rep Row 5.

Row 16 (mock popcorn row) (WS): Ch 1 (counts as first sc), sk first sc, 1 sc in BL of next 3 sc, *working in both loops of sts, 1 tr in next st, sc next st; rep from * 14 (16, 18) times more, end 1 tr next st, sc in BL of next 3 sc, 1 sc in tch, turn—16 (19, 22) tr for mock popcorns.

Row 17: Ch 1 (counts as first sc), sk first sc, 1 sc in BL of next 3 sc, sc in each sc and each tr across to last 4 sts, 1 sc in BL of next 3 sc, 1 sc in tch, turn.

Rep Rows 6–17 until piece measures 11½ (13½, 15½)" [29 (34.5, 39.5) cm] from beg.

Shape Right Neck

Row 1: Ch 1 (counts as first sc), sk first sc, sk first st, 1 sc in BL of next 3 sts, working both loops of sts, sc in next 5, (7, 9) sts, sc in BL of next 3 sts, turn, leaving rem sts to be worked later.

Working on the 13 (15, 17) sts, keeping 5 sts at outside edge and 3 sts at neck edge in sc in BL only, and center 5 (7, 9) sts in patt as established, work even until piece measures 3½ (4, 4½)" [9 (10, 11.5) cm] from beg of neck shaping.

Next Row: Ch 1 (counts as first sc), sk first sc, 1 sc in BL of each st across, 1 sc in beg ch, turn—13 (15, 17) sc.

Rep last row for 3 rows more. End off.

Shape Left Neck

Sk 13 (15, 17) sts to the left of last st made in Row 1 of right neck shaping, join yarn in next st, and work left neck shaping on rem 13 (15, 17) sts same as right neck shaping.

Under Belt

With RS facing, join yarn on side edge 3½ (4½, 5½)" [9 (11.5, 14) cm] below beg of left neck shaping, ch 1, sc in each of next 9 (11, 13) row-end sts, turn—10 (12, 14) sts.

Row 1: Ch 1 (counts as first sc), sc in BL of each sc across, sc in top of beg ch, turn.

Rep Row 1 until belt measures 6 (7, 8)" [15 (18, 20.5) cm] from beg. End off.

Finishing

Sew snaps on under belt and neck tabs; sew buttons over snaps.

jumbo christmas stocking

Crochet stitches are usually higher and wider than a comparable knit stitch, so designing these jumbo Christmas stockings meant working them individually to meet the desired finished dimensions. When both stockings were done, I found another surprise awaiting me. As I charted out the embroidery, there was no way to make the letters the same size. Duplicate stitch works beautifully for embroidering letters on knit. For the crocheted stocking, I used cross stitch, charting each single crochet as one block on the graph.

Jumbo Christmas Stocking

Knit

YARN

Medium-weight smooth yarn **4 MEDIUM**

Shown: *Canadiana* by Patons, 100% acrylic, 3.5 oz. (100 g)/201 yd. (181 m): cranberry #13 (A), 2 skeins; aran #104 (B), 1 skein

NEEDLES

Size 6 (4 mm)

Size 8 (5 mm) double-pointed needles (dpn) or sizes to obtain correct gauge

STITCHES

Stockinette stitch

Ribbing stitch

GAUGE

15 sts = 4" (10 cm)

Take time to check gauge.

NOTIONS/SUPPLIES

Stitch holders

Tapestry needle

SIZE

25" (63.5 cm) from cuff to heel

Cuff

Note: Cuff and body are worked back and forth in rows. After turning heel, foot and toe are worked in the round.

With size 6 needles and B, cast on 76 sts.

Row 1: *K2, p2, rep from * across.

Rep Row 1 until cuff is 5" (12.5 cm) long.

Body

Change to size 8 needles and A. Work stockinette st (knit 1 row, purl 1 row) for 13" (33 cm) more.

Shape Heel

Sl first 19 sts onto a dpn (half of heel sts), sl next 38 sts on holder to be worked later for instep, sl rem 19 onto another dpn (other half of heel). End off A.

Place 38 heel sts onto one needle, join B, work as follows:

Next row (WS): Purl.

Next row: Knit

Rep last 2 rows until heel measures 3" (7.5 cm).

Turn Heel

K23, turn.

Sl1, p10, turn.

Sl1, k9, k2tog, k1, turn.

Sl1, p10, p2tog, p1, turn.

Sl1, k11, k2tog, k1, turn.

Sl1, p12, p2tog, p1, turn.

Sl1, k13, k2tog, k1, turn.

Sl1, p14, p2tog, p1 turn.

Sl 1, k15, k2tog, k1, turn.

Sl1, p16, p2tog, p1, turn.

Sl1, k17, k2tog, k1, turn.

Sl1, p18, p2tog, p5—28 sts. End off B. Join A.

Foot

Using size 8 dpn, with right side facing, k28 heel sts, pick up 8 sts along one side of heel (this will be called first needle); with second needle, k38 sts from holder for instep; with 3rd needle, pick up 8 sts along other side of heel; k14 sts from first needle onto third needle. Join, begin working in rounds (knit every row)—you will now have sts divided onto 3 needles, with center of heel being beg of each round. There are 22 sts on first needle, 38 sts on second needle, 22 sts on third needle—82 sts.

Working in rounds, dec instep as follows:

Rnd 1: K to within 3 sts at end of first needle, k2tog, k1, k across second needle; on third needle, k1, sl1, k1, psso, k to end of third needle.

Rnd 2: Knit.

Rep Rnds 1 and 2 until there are 19 sts on first and third needles and 38 sts on second needle.

Cont working in the round until A measures 5" (12.5 cm) from bottom of heel. End off A. Start B and join at beg of first needle.

Toe Shaping

Rnd 1: Knit all sts.

Rnd 2: First needle, k to last 3 sts, k2tog, k1; second needle, k1, sl1, k1, psso, k to last 3 sts, k2tog, k1; third needle, k1, sl1, k1, psso, k to end.

Rep Rnds 1 and 2 until 24 sts rem, 6 sts on first needle, 12 sts on second needle, 6 sts on third needle. Knit the 6 sts from first needle onto third, you now have 2 needles with 12 sts on each. Weave these stitches together to form toe closing. (Refer to Grafting on page 119.)

Hanging Loop

Made with a twisted cord. Before starting cord, cut an 8" (20.5 cm) length of yarn and set aside for tying. Cut a length of yarn 24" (61 cm) long, fold in half, anchor one end, twist over and over until tightly twisted. Fold in half again, being sure not to let go of ends, allow to twist, tie one end. Trim, sew inside cuff to form loop for hanging stocking.

Embroidery

Following the chart provided on page 85, using duplicate stitch embroidery, embroider initials or a name and decorative pattern onto the stocking.

Finishing

Sew back seam.

Blocking: Lay stocking on a padded surface, spritz lightly with water, pat into shape, and allow to dry.

(continued)

Jumbo Christmas Stocking (continued)

knit

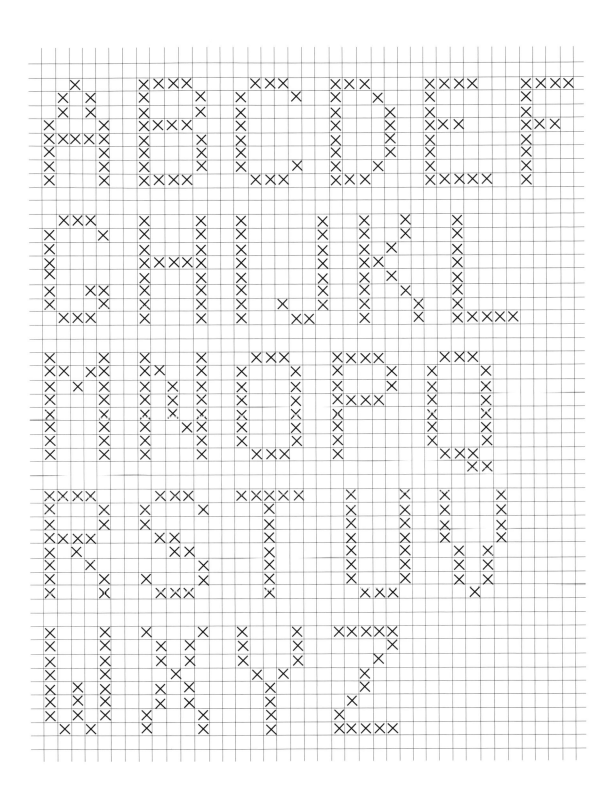

Jumbo Christmas Stocking

crochet

YARN

Medium-weight smooth yarn

Shown: *Canadiana* by Patons, 100% acrylic, 3.5 oz. (100 g)/201 yd. (181 m): cranberry #13 (A), 2 skeins; aran #104 (B), 1 skein

HOOKS

Size G-6 (4 mm)

Size H-8 (5 mm) or sizes to obtain correct gauge

STITCHES

Chain stitch

Slip stitch

Single crochet

GAUGE

14 sts = 4" (10 cm) with H-8 hook

Take time to check gauge.

NOTIONS/SUPPLIES

Tapestry needle

Stitch markers or yarn scraps for markers

SIZE

25" (63.5 cm) from cuff to toe with cuff folded down

Cuff

Notes:

1. Sc2tog: Insert hook in next st, yo, draw yarn through st, insert hook in next st, yo, draw yarn through st, yo, draw yarn through 3 lps on hook.

2. Cuff is worked separately from side to side. Body is joined to cuff and worked back and forth in rows.

With size G-6 hook, and B, ch 22. Foundation row: Starting in 2nd ch from hook, work 1 sc in each ch across, turn—21 sc.

Row 1: Ch 1 (counts as sc) skip first sc, working in BL of sts, work 1 sc in each of next 19 sc, 1 sc in top of tch, turn—21 sts.

Rep Row 1 until 56 rows have been completed (28 ridges). End off B.

Body

Row 1 (RS): With H-8 hook, join A in first row-end st on one long edge of cuff, ch 1, sk first row, 1 sc in each row-end st across one long edge of cuff, turn—56 sts.

Row 2 (WS): Ch 1 (counts as sc), sk first sc, *1 sc in BL of next sc, rep from * across, 1 sc in top of tch, turn.

Row 3: Ch 1 (counts as first sc) sk first sc, *1 sc in FL of next sc, rep from * across, 1 sc in top of tch, turn.

Rep Rows 2 and 3 until Body measures 13" (33 cm) from Cuff. End off A.

Begin Heel

With RS facing, join B 14 sts to right of center back, working in both lps of sts, ch 1, sc in next 27 sts, turn—28 sts.

Working in both lps of sts, work even in sc until Heel measures 3" (7.5 cm) from beg.

Shape Heel

Row 1: Ch 1 (counts as first sc), sk first st, sc in each of next 22 sts, turn, leaving 5 sts at end not worked.

Row 2: Ch 1 (counts as first sc), sk first st, sc in each of next 17 sts, turn, leaving 5 sts at end not worked.

Row 3: Ch 1 (counts as first sc), sk first st, sc in each of next 12 sts, turn, leaving 5 sts at end not worked—8 sts. End off B.

Foot

Note: Foot is worked in rounds. For pattern to match upper part of stocking, it is necessary to join each round with a sl st and turn. Cont in patt as established for body of stocking, carrying up markers after each round.

Rnd 1: With RS facing, sk first 4 sts on last row of Heel, join A in next sc, ch 1 (counts as first sc), sc next3 sc, sc in next 5 skipped sc in next row, sc in next 5 skipped sc in next row, work 9 sc evenly spaced across side of Heel, place marker in work, sc in FL of next 28 sc, place marker in work, work 9 sc evenly spaced across side of Heel, sc in each of next 5 skipped sts, sc in each of next 5 skipped sts in next row, sc in each next 4 sc in next row, sl st in first ch to join, turn—74 sts.

Dec for instep as follows:

Rnd 2 (dec rnd): Ch 1 (counts as first sc), sk first ch, working in BL of sts, sc in each st across to within 2 sts before first marker, sc2tog in next 2 sts, bring up marker, sc in each of next 28 sc, bring up

marker, sc2tog in next 2 sts, sc in each of last 12 sts, sl st in first st to join, turn—72 sts.

Rep Rnd 2 until there are 14 sts on each heel side and 28 sts across instep—56 sts total. Work even in sc rnds until Foot measures 6" (15 cm) from bottom of Heel. End A, join B.

Shape Toe

Rnd 1: Ch 1 (counts as first sc), sk first ch, sc in next 11 sts, sc2tog in next 2 sts, bring up marker, sc2tog in next 2 sts, sc in next 24 sts, sc2tog in next 2 sts, bring up marker, sc2tog in next 2 sts, sc in last 12 sts, sl st in first st to join, turn—4 dec made; 52 sts.

Work 1 rnd even on 52 sts, bringing up markers as you work, sl st in first st to join, turn

Next rnd: Ch 1 (counts as first sc), sc in next 10 sts, sc2tog in next 2 sts, bring up marker, sc2tog in next 2 sts, sc in next 22 sts, sc2tog in next 2 sts, bring up marker, sc2tog in next 2 sts, sc in last 11 sts, sl st in first st to join, turn.

Work 1 rnd even on 48 sts, bringing up markers as you work, sl st in first st to join.

Rep last 2 rnds, dec 1 st before and after each marker, every other rnd until 12 sts rem. End off B leaving a yarn length. With yarn needle weave yarn length through sts in last rnd, gather and secure for toe end.

Hanging Cord

Using yarn double-stranded, ch 24. End off leaving a sewing length. Sew both ends to inside of cuff, at back of stocking for hanging loop.

Embroidery

Using the chart on page 85, cross-stitch initials or name and pattern.

Finishing

Sew back seam.

Blocking: Lay stocking on a padded surface, spritz with water, pat into shape, and allow to dry.

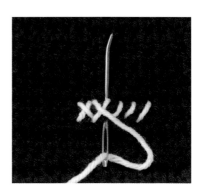

woven plaid placemats

Customize your table setting with handmade placemats, choosing colors to coordinate with your dinnerware. In swatching openwork patterns for the placemats, I found out a few surprising things. I thought that this was going to be one of the easier ones to get a knit/crochet look alike, but it was not. After a few tries, I found something that worked. By using a half double crochet over the post of a single crochet, I was able to duplicate the look of the knitted garter and yarn-over stitches. The other surprise was that I got the exact same gauge in both the knitted and crocheted versions, even though the crocheted one is slightly heavier.

Woven Plaid Placemats

knit

YARN

Lightweight smooth yarn

Shown: *Grace* by Patons, 100% cotton, 1.8 oz. (50 g)/136 yd. (122 m): natural #6008 (A), 8 skeins; taupe #60012 (B), 1 skein; terracotta #60604 (C), 1 skein (makes 4 placemats)

NEEDLES

Size 6 (4 mm) or size to obtain correct gauge

STITCHES

Knit
Purl
Picot bind-off (for flower)

GAUGE

19½ sts = 4" (10 cm)
Take time to check gauge.

NOTIONS/SUPPLIES

Rustproof pins for blocking
Tapestry needle

SIZE

14" x 19½" (35.5 x 49.5 cm)

Placemat

Notes:

1. Yarn-over stitches have a tendency to knit on the bias but blocking will correct this.

2. The slipped stitch at the beginning of every row makes a nice beaded edging.

Cast on 70 sts.

Row 1 (RS): Sl1, k across row.

Rows 2–5: Sl1, k across row.

Row 6: Sl1, k4, p to last 5, k5.

Rows 7 and 8: Rep Row 6.

Row 9 (RS): Sl1, k4, *yo, sl1, k1, psso, rep from * to last 5, k5.

Rep Rows 6–9 till piece measures 18½" (47 cm), ending with Row 8.

Rep Rows 1–5.

Bind off in knit.

Leaf

Make 3.

With col B, cast on 9 sts.

Row 1: Purl.

Row 2: K4, yo, k1, yo, k4—11 sts.

Row 3: Purl.

Row 4: K1, sl1, k1, psso, k2, yo, k1, yo, k2 , k2tog, k1.

Row 5: Purl.

Row 6: K1, sl1, k1, psso, k2, yo, k1, yo, k2, k2tog, k1.

Row 7: Purl.

Row 8: K1, sl1, k1, psso, k2, yo, k1, yo, k2, k2tog, k1.

Row 9: P1, p2tog, p to last 3 sts, p2tog, p1–9 sts.

Row 10: K1, sl1, k1, psso, k1, yo, k1, yo, k1, k2tog, k1.

Row 11: P1, p2tog, p3, p2tog, p1–7 sts.

Row 12: K1, sl1, k1, psso, yo, k1, yo, k2tog, k1.

Row 13: Purl.

Row 14: K1, sl1, k1 psso, yo, k1, yo, k2tog, k1.

Row 15: P1, p2tog, p1, p2tog, p1–5 sts.

Row 16: K2tog, yo, k1, yo, k2tog.

Row 17: P2tog, p1, p2tog—3 sts.

Row 18: K3.

Row 19: P3tog. Fasten off last st.

Flower

With col C, cast on 10 sts.

Row 1: K in back, front, and back again of each st—30 sts.

Row 2: Knit.

Row 3: *K1, inc in next st, rep from * across row—45 sts.

Row 4: Knit.

Bind off using picot bind off as follows:

Bind off 2 sts, *slip the st that remains on the right-hand needle back onto left-hand needle, cast on 2 sts, bind off 4 sts; rep from * to end, fasten off.

Finishing

Block to shape by pinning on a padded surface, spritz with water, pat into shape, allow to dry thoroughly. After piece is dry, weave color stripes as follows:

To form the vertical woven stripes, cut 3 strands of C, each 50" (127 cm) long. Thread all three strands on tapestry needle. Starting at bottom, in the seventh hole from left side, start weaving in and out of holes, when you reach the top, skip one hole, work from top to bottom the same, skip one hole, work back up to top—3 vertical stripes worked in C, end off C, leaving a 3" (7.5 cm) end to weave in.

Cut 3 strands of B, each 38" (96.5 cm) long, work the skipped holes the same.

To form the horizontal woven stripes, cut 3 strands of C, each 2 yd. (1.8 m) long. Starting at left edge, in the third hole up from bottom, work in the same way, anchoring the vertical strips as you weave.

Sew the flower and leaves on upper left corner, using the photo as a guide.

Note: The Cibi bent end tapestry needle works very well for finishing work on both knitted and crocheted projects, like seams and weaving in loose ends. It's also perfect for weaving the yarns through these placemats. The curved tip helps maneuver the needle accurately and quickly.

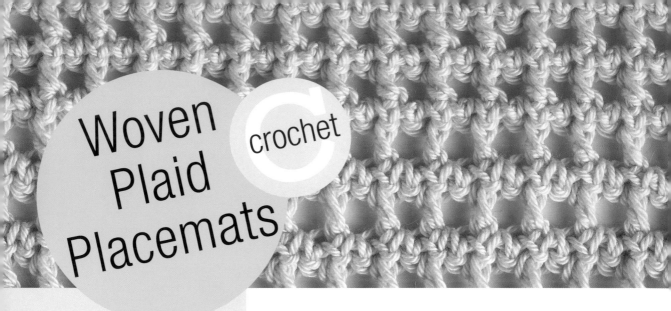

Woven Plaid Placemats

crochet

YARN

Lightweight smooth yarn

Shown: *Grace* by Patons, 100% cotton, 1.8 oz. (50 g)/136 yd. (122 m): natural #6008 (A), 8 skeins; taupe #60012 (B), 1 skein; terracotta #60604 (C), 1 skein (makes 4 placemats)

HOOK

Size G-6 (4 mm) or size to obtain correct gauge

STITCHES

Single crochet
Half double crochet
Front post hdc
Reverse sc

GAUGE

19 sts = 4" (10 cm)
Take time to check gauge.

NOTIONS/SUPPLIES

Rustproof pins for blocking
Tapestry needle

SIZE

14" x 20" (35.5 x 51 cm)

Placemat

Note: Front post hdc (FPhdc): Yo, insert hook from front to back around the post of next sc, yo, draw yarn through, yo, draw yarn through 3 loops on hook.

With A, ch 70.
Foundation row (WS): Hdc in 3rd ch from hook, 1 hdc in each ch across, turn—69 hdc.

Row 1: Ch 2 (counts as first hdc), sk first st, working in BL only, 1 hdc in each hdc across, hdc in top of tch, turn.

Row 2: Rep Row 1.

Row 3: Ch 2 (counts as first hdc), sk first st, 1 hdc in BL of next 4 hdc, *working in both loops of sts, ch 1, sk next hdc, 1 dc in next hdc, rep from * 28 times more, ch 1, sk next hdc, 1 hdc in BL of next 4 hdc, 1 hdc in top of tch, turn—30 ch-1 spaces, 5 hdc on each side for border sts.

Row 4: Ch 1 (counts as first sc), sk first hdc, sc in BL of next 4 hdc, *working in both loops of sts, 1 sc in next ch-1 space, 1 sc in next hdc, rep from * 28 times, 1 sc in last ch-1 space, 1 sc in BL in next 4 hdc, 1 sc in top of tch, turn.

Row 5: Ch 2 (counts as first hdc), sk first sc, 1 hdc in BL in next 4 sc *ch 1, sk next sc, 1 FPhdc around the post of next sc, rep from * 28 times, ch 1, sk next sc, 1 hdc in BL of next 4 sc, 1 hdc in the tch, turn—30 ch-1 spaces.

Rep Rows 4 and 5 until placemat measures 18½" (47 cm) from beg, ending with Row 4 of pattern.

Working in BL only, work 3 rows even in hdc. End off.

Leaf

Make 3.

With B, ch 16.

Row 1: 5 dc in 4th ch from hook, 1 dc in each of next 4 ch, 1 hdc in each of next 4 ch, 1 sc in each of next 3 ch (1 sc, ch 3, 1 sc), in last ch. Working across opposite side of foundation ch, 1 sc in each of next 3 ch, 1 hdc in each of next 4 ch, 1 dc in each of next 4 ch (5 dc, ch 3, sc), in next ch. End off.

Flower

With C, ch 12.

Foundation row: Work 2 dc in 3rd ch from hook (2 skipped ch count as dc), work 3 dc in each ch across, turn—30 dc.

Row 1 (picot row): *Ch 3, 1 sc in 3rd ch from hook for picot, sc next dc, rep from * across—30 picots. End off.

Finishing

Block to shape by pinning on a padded surface, spritz with water, pat into shape, allow to dry thoroughly.

Edging

Rnd 1: With RS facing, join A in first st to the left of any corner, ch 1, sc evenly around, sl st in beg ch to join.

Rnd 2: Ch 1, working from left to right, reverse sc in each sc around, sl st in beg ch to join.

Weave the stripes and attach the flower and leaves on the upper left corner.

Bouclé pillow

Decorative pillows can add a dash of color to any room. Use a beautiful designer yarn and simple stitches to create these great pillows. The gauge was very close for both the knit and crochet versions, but as in some other projects, I doubled the finer yarn in the knitted stitches in order to get a similar gauge.

Bouclé Pillow

Knit

YARN

Medium-weight smooth yarn

Shown: *Petite Beaded Cotton Rayon* by Blue Heron Yarns, 50% rayon, 50% cotton, 8 oz. (227 g)/250 yd. (229 m): melon (A), 1 skein

Medium-weight bouclé yarn

Shown: *Rayon Loop* by Blue Heron Yarns, 100% rayon, 8 oz. (227 g)/325 yd. (297 m): day lily (B), 1 skein

NEEDLES

Size 8 (5 mm) or size to obtain correct gauge

STITCHES

Stockinette stitch
Garter stitch

GAUGE

9 sts = 4" (10 cm) when stretched
Take time to check gauge.

NOTIONS/SUPPLIES

Tapestry needle
14" (35.5 cm) pillow form
1⅞" (4.8 cm) half ball cover button
5" (12.5 cm) doll needle

SIZE

14" x 14" (35.5 x 35.5 cm)

Pillow

Note: Petite Beaded Cotton Rayon is used double-stranded throughout. When winding skein, wind into two balls.

Make 2 pieces.

With A, cast on 142 sts.

Rows 1–4: Knit every row.

Row 5: K, dec 10 sts evenly spaced across row—132 sts.

Row 6 (WS): Knit.

Row 7: Knit.

Row 8 (dec row): K15, *k3tog, k30, rep from * 2 times more, k3tog, k15—124 sts. Drop A, pick up B.

Row 9: With B, knit.

Row 10: P14, *p3tog, p28, rep from * 2 times more, p3tog, p14—116 sts.

Row 11: Knit.

Row 12: P13, *p3tog, p26, rep from * 2 times more, p3tog, p13—108 sts. Drop B, pick up A.

Row 13: With A, knit.

Row 14: K12, *k3tog, k24, rep from * 2 times more, k3tog, p12—100 sts.

Row 15: Knit.

Row 16: K11, *k3tog, k22, rep from * 2 times more, k3tog, k11—92 sts. Drop A, pick up B.

Row 17: With B, knit.

Row 18: P10, *p3tog, p20, rep from * 2 times more, p3tog, p10—84 sts.

Row 19: Knit.

Row 20: P9, *p3tog, p18, rep from * 2 times more, p3tog, p9—76 sts. Drop B, pick up A.

Row 21: With A, knit.

Row 22: K8, *k3tog, k16, rep from * 2 times more, k3tog, k8—68 sts.

Row 23: Knit.

Row 24: K7, *k3tog, k14, rep from * 2 times more, k3tog, k7—60 sts. Drop A, pick up B.

Row 25: With B, knit.

Row 26: P6, *p3tog, p12, rep from * 2 times more, p3tog, p6—52 sts.

Row 27: Knit.

Row 28: P5, *p3tog, p10, rep from * 2 times more, p3tog, p5—44 sts. Drop B, pick up A.

Row 29: With A, knit.

Row 30: K4, *k3tog, k8, rep from * 2 times more, k3tog, k4—36 sts.

Row 31: Knit.

Row 32: K3, *k3tog, k6, rep from * 2 times more, k3tog, k3—28 sts. Drop A, pick up B.

Row 33: With B, knit.

Row 34: P2, *p3tog, p4, rep from * 2 times more, p3tog, p2—20 sts.

Row 35: Knit.

Row 36: P1, *p3tog, p2, rep from * 2 times more, p3tog, p1—12 sts. Drop B, pick up A.

Row 37: With A, knit.

Row 38: K2tog across row—6 sts.

Row 39: K2tog across row—3 sts.

Row 40: K3tog; end off.

Finishing

Sew center seam of both pieces.

With right sides together, sew 3 sides of squares together, turn right side out, place pillow form inside this pocket; it should be tightly drawn over the pillow form. Sew remaining side.

Tassels

Make 4.

Before starting tassel, cut 2 strands of A, each 30" (76 cm) long, to be used for tying tassels. Using a 7½" (19 cm) piece of cardboard, one strand each of A and B, wrap around cardboard 25 times. Place one tying strand under the top of the tassel and tie a secure knot,

leaving long tails. Cut the bottom of the tassel. Tie the second tying strand securely around the tassel, about 1¾" (3 cm) from the top. Draw the ends into the lower part of the tassel and trim off. Use top ends to secure tassel to corner of pillow, then draw through the knot to become part of tassel.

Covered Button

Make one.

Using 2 strands of B, cast on 4 sts.

Row 1: Knit, inc 1 st in each st— 8 sts.

Row 2: Knit, inc 1 st in each st— 16 sts.

Row 3: Knit.

Row 4: *K1, inc 1 st next st, rep from * across row—24 sts.

Row 5: Knit.

Row 6: *K2, inc 1 next st, rep from * across—32 sts.

Rows 7 and 8: Knit.

Bind off, leave a long end for sewing. Sew row ends together forming a circle.

Place button in button cover, catching yarn on teeth of button cover all around. Using the doll needle, attach button to center of pillow, draw yarn through to other side, tie, then go back again to secure tightly.

Bouclé Pillow

crochet

YARN

Medium-weight smooth yarn
Shown: *Petite Beaded Cotton
Rayon* by Blue Heron Yarns,
50% rayon, 50% cotton, 8 oz.
(227 g)/250 yd. (229 m):
melon (A), 1 skein

Medium-weight bouclé yarn
Shown: *Rayon Loop* by Blue Heron
Yarns, 100% rayon, 8 oz.
(227 g)/325 yd. (297 m):
day lily (B), 1 skein

HOOKS

Size H-8 (5 mm) or size to
obtain correct gauge

STITCHES

Chain stitch
Slip stitch
Single crochet

GAUGE

13 sts = 4" (10 cm) when
stretched; first 12 rnds = 3½"
(9 cm) in diameter
Take time to check gauge.

NOTIONS/SUPPLIES

Tapestry needle
14" (35.5 cm) pillow form
1⅞"(4.8 cm) half ball cover button
5" (12.5 cm) doll needle

SIZE

14" x 14" (35.5 x 35.5 cm)

Pillow

Notes

*1. Sc2tog: Insert hook in next st, yo,
draw yarn through st, insert hook in
next st, yo, draw yarn through st, yo,
draw yarn through 3 lps on hook.*

*2. Sc3tog: [Insert hook in next st, yo,
draw yarn through st] 3 times, yo,
draw yarn through 4 lps on hook.*

*3. You are starting at the outside
edge of pillow and dec toward
center to make a square.*

*4. Turning ch 1 always counts as
the first st, sk the first st each time.*

*5. The last st is always the top of
the turning ch from the row below.*

*6. Colors change every 4th row, do
not cut colors, on last sc, draw up
new color for ch 1.*

Make 2 pieces.

With A, ch 135.

Foundation row (WS): 1 sc in
2nd ch from hook, 1 sc in each ch
across, turn—134 sc.

Row 1 (RS): With A, working in BL
of sts, ch 1 (counts as first sc), sk
first st, 1 sc in each of next 132 sc,
1 sc in top of tch, turn—134 sts.

Row 2 (WS): Working in BL of sts,
ch 1 (counts as first sc), 1 sc in each
of the next 19 sc, sc2tog in next 2
sts, 1 sc in each of the next 90 sts,
sc2tog in next 2 sts, 1 sc in next 19
sts, 1 sc in top of tch, turn—132 sc.

Row 3: Working in BL of sts, ch 1,
1 sc in each sc across, 1 sc in top of
tch, turn—132 sc.

Row 4 (dec row): Working in BL
of sts, ch 1 (counts as first sc), sk
first st, 1 sc in each of next 14 sc,
*sc3tog in next 3 sts, 1 sc in next 30
sts; rep from * 2 times more, sc3tog
in next 3 sts, sc in next 14 sts, 1 sc
in top of tch, turn—124 sts. Drop
A, pick up B.

Row 5: With B, working in both lps
of sts, ch 1 (counts as first sc), sk
first st, 1 sc in each st across, 1 sc in
top of tch, turn—124 sts.

Row 6 (dec row): Working in both
lps of sts, ch 1 (counts as first sc), sk
first st, 1 sc in each of next 13 sts,
*sc3tog in next 3 sts, 1 sc in each
of next 28 sts; rep from * 2 times
more, sc3tog in next 3 sts, 1 sc in
each of next 13 sts, 1 sc in top of
tch, turn—116 sts.

Row 7: Working in both lps of sts, rep Row 5—116 sts.

Row 8 (dec row): Working in both lps of sts, ch 1 (counts as first sc), sk first st, 1 sc in each of next 12 sts, *sc3tog in next 3 sts, 1 sc in each of next 26 sts; rep from * 2 times more, sc3tog in next 3 sts, 1 sc in each of next 12 sts, 1 sc in top of tch, turn—108 sts. Drop B, pick up A.

Row 9: Working in both lps of sts, rep Row 5—108 sts.

Row 10 (dec row): With A, working in BL of sts, ch 1 (counts as first sc), sk first st, 1 sc in each of next 11 sts, *sc3tog in next 3 sts, 1 sc in each of next 24 sts; rep from * 2 times more, sc3tog in next 3 sts, 1 sc in each of next 11 sts, 1 sc in top of tch, turn—100 sts.

Row 11: Working in BL of sts, rep Row 5—100 sts.

Row 12 (dec row): Working in BL of sts, ch 1 (counts as first sc), sk first st, 1 sc in each of next 10 sts, *sc3tog in next 3 sts, 1 sc in each of next 22 sts; rep from * 2 times more, sc3tog in next 3 sts, 1 sc in each of next 10 sts, 1 sc in top of tch, turn—92 sts. Drop A, pick up B.

Row 13: With B, working in BL of sts, rep Row 5—92 sts.

Row 14 (dec row): Working in both lps of sts, ch 1 (counts as first sc), sk first st, 1 sc in each of next 9 sts, *sc3tog in next 3 sts, 1 sc in each of next 20 sts; rep from * 2 times more, sc3tog in next 3 sts, 1 sc in each of next 9 sts, 1 sc in top of tch, turn—84 sts.

Row 15: Working in both lps of sts, rep Row 5—84 sts.

Row 16 (dec row): Working in both lps of sts, ch 1 (counts as first sc), sk first st, 1 sc in each of next 8 sts, *sc3tog in next 3 sts, 1 sc in each of next 18 sts; rep from * 2 times more, sc3tog in next 3 sts, 1 sc in each of next 8 sts, 1 sc in top of tch, turn—76 sts. Drop B, pick up A.

Row 17: With A, working in both lps of sts, rep Row 5—76 sts.

Row 18 (dec row): Working in BL of sts, ch 1 (counts as first sc), sk first st, 1 sc in each of next 7 sts, *sc3tog in next 3 sts, 1 sc in each of next 16 sts; rep from * 2 times more, sc3tog in next 3 sts, 1 sc in each of next 7 sts, 1 sc in top of tch, turn—68 sts.

Row 19: Working in BL of sts, rep Row 5—68 sts.

Row 20 (dec row): Working in BL of sts, ch 1 (counts as first sc), sk first st, 1 sc in each of next 6 sts, *sc3tog in next 3 sts, 1 sc in each of next 14 sts; rep from * 2 times more, sc3tog in next 3 sts, 1 sc in each of next 6 sts, 1 sc in top of tch, turn—60 sts. Drop A, pick up B.

Row 21: With B, working in BL of sts, rep Row 5—60 sts.

Row 22 (dec row): Working in both lps of sts, ch 1 (counts as first sc), sk first st, 1 sc in each of next 5 sts, *sc3tog in next 3 sts, 1 sc in each of next 12 sts; rep from * 2 times more, sc3tog in next 3 sts, 1 sc in each of next 5 sts, 1 sc in top of tch, turn—52 sts.

Row 23: Working in both lps of sts, rep Row 5—52 sts.

Row 24 (dec row): Working in both lps of sts, ch 1 (counts as first sc), sk first st, 1 sc in each of next 4 sts, *sc3tog in next 3 sts, 1 sc in each of next 10 sts, rep from * 2 times more, sc3tog in next 3 sts, 1 sc in each of next 4 sts, 1 sc in top of tch, turn—44 sts. Drop B, pick up A.

(continued)

Bouclé Pillow
(continued)

Row 25: With A, working in both loops of sts, rep Row 5—44 sts.

Row 26 (dec row): Working in BL of sts, ch 1 (counts as first sc), sk first st, 1 sc in each of next 3 sts, *sc3tog in next 3 sts, 1 sc in each of next 8 sts; rep from * 2 times more, sc3tog in next 3 sts, 1 sc in each of next 3 sts, 1 sc in top of tch, turn—36 sts.

Row 27: Working in BL of sts, rep Row 5—36 sts.

Row 28 (dec row): Working in BL of sts, ch 1 (counts as first sc), sk first st, 1 sc in each of next 2 sts, *sc3tog in next 3 sts, 1 sc in each of next 6 sts; rep from * 2 times more, sc3tog in next 3 sts, 1 sc in each of next 2 sts, 1 sc in top of tch, turn—28 sts. Drop A, pick up B.

Row 29: With B, working in BL of sts, rep Row 5—28 sts.

Row 30 (dec row): Working in both loops of sts, ch 1 (counts as first sc), sk first st, 1 sc in next st, *sc3tog in next 3 sts, 1 sc in each of next 4 sts; rep from * 2 times more, sc3tog in next 3 sts, 1 sc in next st, 1 sc in top of tch, turn—20 sts.

Row 31: Working in both loops of sts, rep Row 5—20 sts.

Row 32 (dec row): Working in both loops of sts, ch 1 (counts as first sc), sk first st, *sc3tog in next 3 sts, 1 sc in each of next 2 sts; rep from * 2 times more, sc3tog in next 3 sts, 1 sc in top of tch, turn—12 sts. Drop B, pick up A.

Row 33: With A, working in both loops of sts, rep Row 5—12 sts.

Row 34: Working in BL only, ch 1 (counts as first sc), sk first st, 1 sc in next st, *sc2tog in next 2 sts; rep from * across, turn—7 sts.

Row 35: Working in BL only, ch 1 (counts as first sc), sk first st, *sc2tog in next 2 sts; rep from * across, turn—4 sts.

Row 36: Ch 1 (counts as first sc), sc3tog in next 3 sts. End off.

Finishing

Sew center seam of both pieces. With right sides together, sew three sides of squares together, turn right side out, place pillow form inside this pocket; it should be tightly drawn over the pillow form. Sew remaining side.

Tassels

Make tassels as for knitted pillow, page 97.

Covered Button

Make one.

Using 2 strands of B, ch 4, join with a sl st to form a ring.

Rnd 1: Work 8 sc in ring, place marker in work, work in a spiral, moving marker up as work progresses.

Rnd 2: 2 sc in each st around—16 sc.

Rnd 3: *1 sc next st, 2 sc in next st: rep from * around—24 sc.

Rnd 4: *1 sc in each of next 2 sts, 2 sc in next st; rep from * around—32 sc.

Rnd 5: Sc in each sc around, sl st in next sc to join. End off.

Place button in button cover, catching yarn on teeth of button cover all around. Using the doll needle, attach button to center of pillow, draw yarn through to other side, tie, then go back again to secure tightly.

color block afghan

Beautiful, bold colors in an asymmetrical striping pattern make this afghan a striking accent to any home décor. An easy textured stitch, in either knit or crochet, using a wonderful yarn, creates a really plush, modern look. The afghan is worked in three panels, and the pattern is super easy. The Louet *Gems* yarn I used comes in different weights of the same colors. By knitting with worsted weight yarn and crocheting with sport weight yarn, I was able to achieve the same gauge.

Color Block Afghan

K knit

YARN

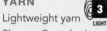

Lightweight yarn
Shown: *Gems* by Louet, 100%
  merino wool worsted weight,
  3.5 oz. (100 g)/175 yd. (165 m):
  burgundy #58 (A), 5 skeins;
  willow #55 (B), 4 skeins;
  crabapple #26 (C), 3 skeins

NEEDLES

Size 6 (4 mm) or size to
  obtain correct gauge

STITCHES

Double seed stitch

GAUGE

18 sts = 4" (10 cm) in pattern
Take time to check gauge.

NOTIONS/SUPPLIES

Tapestry needle

SIZE

49½" x 60" (125.5 x 152.5 cm)

Afghan

Notes:

*1. Afghan is knitted in three panels.
Follow chart (page 107) for changing
colors in each strip.*

*2. When changing colors, omit patt
Row 1, knit across row instead, then
beg Rows 2, 3, and 4.*

Pattern stitch

(multiple of 4 sts + 2)

Row 1: K2, *p2, k2, rep from *
across row.

Row 2: P2, *k2, p2, rep *
across row.

Row 3: P2, *k2, p2, rep from *
across row.

Row 4: K2, *p2, k2, rep from *
across row.

Repeat Rows 1–4 for patt following
chart for color changes for each
panel.

Panels:

Make 3.

Cast on 74 sts. Work in patt st
following a separate chart for
each panel. Bind off.

Finishing

Sew 3 panels together following
chart. Weave in ends.

To preserve texture of pattern,
do not block.

Color Block Afghan crochet

YARN

Fine yarn **2** FINE

Shown: *Gems* by Louet, 100%
merino wool sport weight,
3.5 oz. (100 g)/225 yd. (203 m):
burgundy #58 (A), 6 skeins;
willow #55 (B), 5 skeins;
crabapple #26 (C), 4 skeins

HOOKS

Size G-6 (4 mm) or size to
obtain correct gauge

STITCHES

Chain stitch
Single crochet
Double crochet

GAUGE

15 sts = 4" (10 cm) in
pattern stitch
Take time to check gauge.

NOTIONS/SUPPLIES

Tapestry needle

SIZE

49½" x 60" (125.5 x 152.5 cm)

Afghan

*Notes: Afghan is crocheted in three
strips. Follow chart for changing
colors in each strip.*

With first color in panel, ch 67.

Foundation row: Starting in 2nd ch
from hook, work 1 dc, *1 sc next
ch, 1 dc in next ch; rep from *
across, ending with 1 dc in last ch,
turn—
66 sc.

Row 1: Ch 1 (counts as first sc), sk
first dc, 1 dc in next sc, *1 sc in
next dc, 1 dc in next sc, rep from
* across, ending with last dc in top
of tch, turn—66 sts.

Rep Row 1, following the chart
for color changes.

Finishing

Sew 3 panels together following
chart. Weave in ends.

To preserve texture of pattern,
do not block.

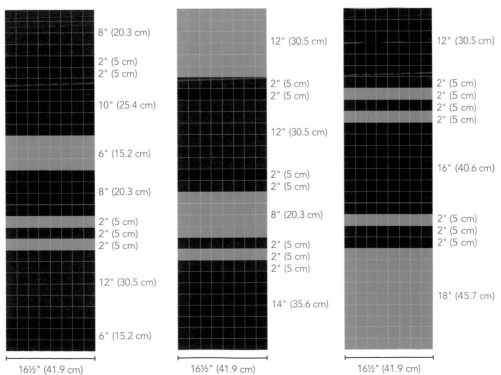

8" (20.3 cm)

2" (5 cm)
2" (5 cm)

10" (25.4 cm)

6" (15.2 cm)

8" (20.3 cm)

2" (5 cm)
2" (5 cm)
2" (5 cm)

12" (30.5 cm)

6" (15.2 cm)

16½" (41.9 cm)

12" (30.5 cm)

2" (5 cm)
2" (5 cm)

12" (30.5 cm)

2" (5 cm)
2" (5 cm)

8" (20.3 cm)

2" (5 cm)
2" (5 cm)
2" (5 cm)

14" (35.6 cm)

16½" (41.9 cm)

12" (30.5 cm)

2" (5 cm)
2" (5 cm)
2" (5 cm)
2" (5 cm)

16" (40.6 cm)

2" (5 cm)
2" (5 cm)
2" (5 cm)

18" (45.7 cm)

16½" (41.9 cm)

Needle and Hook cases

Whether you knit or crochet or do both, you'll enjoy making these colorful holders for your special needles and hooks. Cotton yarn in bright colors makes them cheerful, sturdy, and useful. They also make wonderful gifts for your friends who knit and crochet. Contrasting bands of pockets hold the needles and hooks in place. Store knitting needles or Tunisian hooks in the larger case. Use the smaller case to hold crochet hooks or double-pointed knitting needles.

ChiaoGoo bamboo needles and hooks shown courtesy of Westingbrooke LLC.

Needle and Hook Cases

YARN

Medium-weight yarn

Shown: *Cotton Classic II* by Tahki, 100% cotton, 1.75 oz. (50 g)/74 yd. (67 m): bright lime #2726 (A), 3 skeins; periwinkle #2882 (B), 2 skeins; light turquoise #2815 (C), 2 skeins

NEEDLES

Size 6 (4 mm) or size to obtain correct gauge

STITCHES

Knit
Purl
Slip stitches

GAUGE

20¾ sts = 4" (10 cm)
Take time to check gauge.

NOTIONS/SUPPLIES

Safety pin
Tapestry needle

SIZE

Large case: 15½" x 16" (39.5 x 40.5 cm)
Small case: 8½" x 9" (21.5 x 23 cm)

Large Case

Note: Do not cut yarn at end of rows; carry inactive yarn up sides.

With A, cast on 83 sts. Work garter st (knit every row) for 4 rows.

Begin patt as follows:

Row 1 (RS): With B, *k1, sl1, rep from * across row, end k1.

Row 2: With B, k1, *yf (yarn front), sl1, yb (yarn back), k1, rep from * to end.

Rows 3 and 4: With B, knit.

Row 5: With A, k2, *sl1, k1, rep from * across row, end k2.

Row 6: With A, k2, *yf, sl1, yb, k1, rep from * across row, end k2.

Rows 7 and 8: With A, knit.

Rows 9–12: With C, rep Rows 1–4.

Rep patt Rows 1–12 until 15" (38 cm) from beg.

With A, work garter st for 4 rows. Bind off in knit.

Side Borders

Before beginning side borders, place a pin at center.

With A and right side facing, pick up and k35 sts to marker, then 35 sts on other side of marker. Work 70 sts as follows:

Row 1: Purl.

Row 2: Knit.

Row 3: Knit.

Row 4: Knit.

Row 5: Purl.

Row 6: Knit.

Row 7: Purl.

Bind off in knit.

Work other side the same.

Needle Bands

Make 2.

Note: First row is top of band.

With A, cast on 60 sts. Work as follows:

Row 1 (RS): Knit.

Row 2: Purl.

Row 3: P4, *cast on 5 sts, p4, rep from * 13 times more.

Row 4: K4, *p5 cast on sts, k4, rep from * 13 times more.

Row 5: P4, *k5, p4, rep from * 13 times more.

Row 6: K4, *p5, k4, rep from * 13 times more.

Row 7: P4, *ssk, k1, k2tog, p4, rep from * 13 times more.

Row 8: K4, *p3, k4, rep from *
13 times more.

Row 9: P4, *sl 2, k1, pass both sl
sts over k st, p4, rep from *
13 times more.

Row 10: Knit.

Bind off in purl.

Finishing

Pin Needle Bands in place on
wrong side, first one 4" (10 cm)
from bottom, second one 4" (10
cm) from the first.

Sew bands in place.

Fold the Side Borders to inside
covering the ends of the Needle
Band and hiding the yarns that
were carried up the sides. Sew
Borders in place.

Tie

With A, make a twisted cord
as follows:

Before beginning, cut 2 strands
of yarn 12" (30.5 cm) long, set
aside to be used to tie strands.
Using one strand of yarn, 4 yd.
(3.5 m) long, fold in half, and
anchor the folded end. Twist and
twist these strands until they
become very tightly wound. Being
sure not to let go of ends, bring
both ends together, hold up and
allow to twist into a cord. Tie each
side tightly, about 3" (7.5 cm) from
ends, forming tassels; trim ends.
Pull tie through a stitch at center
of one side.

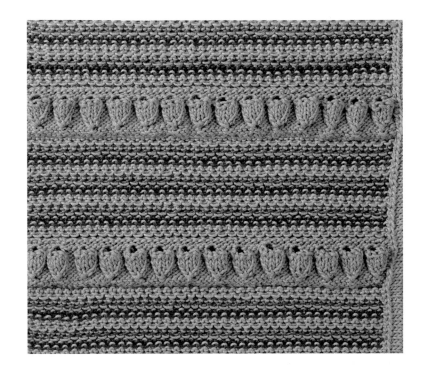

Needle and Hook Cases (continued)

Small Case

With A, cast on 37 sts.

Knit 4 rows.

Rep patt Row 1–12 of large case until 7½" (19 cm).

Knit 4 rows.

Bind off.

Side Border

With A and right side facing, pick up 35 stitches. Work same as side border of large case. Repeat for other side.

Hook Band

Make 1.

Cast on 28 sts.

Rows 1–9: Work Rows 1–9 as for knitting needle case band.

Row 10: *K3, k2tog, rep from * 5 times more, end k4—18 sts.

Rep Rows 3 thru 10.

Bind off in purl.

Finishing

Center band on wrong side and sew in place. Finish side borders as for large case. Using 3 yd. (2.75 m) strand of yarn, make Tie as for large case. Attach at center of one side.

Needle and Hook Cases

crochet

YARN

Medium-weight yarn [4 MEDIUM]

Shown: *Cotton Classic II* by Tahki, 100% cotton, 1.75 oz. (50 g)/74 yd. (67 m): bright lime #2726 (A), 3 skeins; periwinkle #2882 (B), 2 skeins; light turquoise #2815 (C), 2 skeins

HOOKS

Size G-6 (4 mm) or size to obtain correct gauge

STITCHES

Chain stitch

Slip stitch

Single crochet

Pocket stitch: (1 sc, 1 hdc, 3 dc) around the post of same dc

GAUGE

16 sts in (sc, ch 1) pattern = 4" (10 cm)

Take time to check gauge.

NOTIONS/SUPPLIES

Safety pins

Tapestry needle

SIZE

Large case: 15½" x 16" (39.5 x 40.5 cm)

Small case: 8½" x 9" (21.5 x 23 cm)

Large Case

Note: Do not cut inactive yarns; instead, carry them up the side.

With A, ch 65.

Foundation row: Starting in 2nd ch from hook, 1 sc in each ch across, turn—64 sc.

Row 1: Ch 1, sk first st, working in BL only, 1 sc in each of next 62 sc, 1 sc in top of tch, turn—64 sts. Drop A, join B.

Row 2: With B, ch 2 (counts as sc, ch 1), sk first 2 sc, 1 sc in next sc, *ch 1, sk next sc, 1 sc next sc; rep from * across, ending with 1 sc in top of tch, turn—32 ch-1 sps.

Row 3: With B, ch 1, (counts as sc), sk first sc, *1 sc next ch-1 sp, ch 1, sk next sc; rep from * across, ending with 1 sc in last ch-1 sp, 1 sc in top of tch, turn—31 ch-1 sps. Drop B, pick up A from previous row.

Row 4: With A, ch 2 (counts as sc, ch 1), sk first 2 sc, *sc in next ch-1 sp, ch 1, sk next sc; rep from * across, ending with 1 sc in top of tch, turn—32 ch-1 sps.

Row 5: With A, ch 1, (counts as sc), sk first sc, *1 sc next ch-1 sp, ch 1, sk next sc; rep from * across, ending with 1 sc in last ch-1 sp, 1 sc in top of tch, turn—31 ch-1 sps. Drop A, join C.

Rows 6–65: Rep Rows 4–5, working in the following color sequence throughout: 2 rows C, 2 rows B, 2 rows A.

Next Row: With A, ch 1 (counts as sc), sk first sc, working in both loops of st, sc in each sc and each ch-1 sp across, ending with sc in top of tch, turn.

Last Row: With A, ch 1 (counts as sc), sk first sc, working in BL only, sc in each sc across, ending with sc in top of tch. End off.

Side Borders

Before beginning side borders, place a pin at 4" (10 cm) intervals across each side edge as markers for picking up stitches.

First Side Border:

Row 1 (RS): With RS facing, join A in bottom right-hand corner, ch 1 (counts as first sc), work 55 sc evenly spaced across side edge, having 14 sc between each marker, turn.

Needle and Hook Cases (continued)

Row 2: Ch 1 (counts as first sc), sk first sc, working in both loops of sts, sc in each sc across, sc in top of tch. End off.

Second Side Border:

Starting in top left-hand corner, with A, working over carried yarn, rep First Side Border across other side edge.

Needle Bands

Make 2.

With A, ch 58.

Foundation row: Starting in 2nd ch from hook, 1 sc in each ch across, turn—58 sts.

Row 1 (WS): Ch 3 (counts as first dc), sk first sc, 1 dc in each of the next 55 sc, 1 dc in tch, turn—57 sts.

Row 2 (RS): Ch 1 (counts as first sc), sk first dc, [1 sc, 1 hdc, 3 dc] around the post of next dc (pocket st complete), sk next 2 dc, sl st in each of next 2 dc, *[1 sc, 1 hdc, 3 dc] around the post of same dc holding last sl st, sk next 2 dc, 1 sl st in each of next 2 dc; rep from * across, ending with 1 sc in top of tch, turn—14 pocket sts.

Row 3: Ch 3 (counts as first dc), working in Row 1 sts, sk first st, 1 dc in each st across, 1 dc in top of tch, turn—57 sts.

Row 4: Ch 1 (counts as first sc), sk first dc, 1 sc in each dc across, 1 sc in top of tch. End off.

Finishing

Using photo as a guide, sew strips to inside of case.

Tie

With 2 strands of A, ch 110. End off, leaving a 2" (5 cm) end to become part of fringe. Cut seven 4" (10 cm) strands of A. Draw 3 strands through same end of tie to complete first fringe. Draw 4 strands through other end of tie for fringe. Tie an overhand knot at base of each fringe to secure.

Draw Tie through stitches on right-hand side edge near the center

Small Case

With A, ch 35. Work same as large case until 26 rows have been competed before working last 2 rows.

First Side Border:

Row 1 (RS): With RS facing, join A in bottom right-hand corner, ch 1 (counts as first sc), work 28 sc evenly spaced across side edge, turn.

Row 2: Ch 1 (counts as first sc), sk first sc, working in both loops of sts, sc in each sc across, sc in top of tch. End off.

Second Side Border:

Starting in top left-hand corner, with A, working over carried yarn, rep First Side Border across other side edge.

Row 3: Ch 1 (counts as first sc), sk first dc, [1 sc, 1 hdc, 3 dc] around the post of next dc (pocket st complete), sk next 2 dc, sl st in each of next 2 dc, *[1 sc, 1 hdc, 3 dc] around the post of same dc holding last sl st, sk next 2 dc, 1 sl st in each of next 2 dc; rep from * across, ending with 1 sc in top of tch, turn—6 pocket sts.

Row 4: Working in sts of Row 2, ch 3 (counts as first dc), sk first sc, 1 dc in each of next 24 sc, 1 dc in top of tch, turn—26 sts.

Rows 5–8: Rep Rows 1–4. End off.

Tie

With 2 strands of A, ch 80. Finish same as large case tie. Draw Tie stitches on right-hand side edge near the center.

Hook Band

Make 1.

With A ch 26.

Foundation row: Starting in 2nd ch from hook, 1 sc in each ch across, turn—26 sts.

Row 1 (RS): Ch 3 (counts as first dc), sk first sc, 1 dc in each of next 24 sc, 1 dc in top of tch, turn—26 sts.

Row 2: Ch 3 (counts as first dc), sk first sc, 1 dc in each of next 24 sc, 1 dc in top of tch, turn—26 sts.

Knitting Techniques

Knit into the Front and Back

This increase is sometimes called a bar increase because a visible, horizontal bar is formed on the right side of the work.

1. Knit a stitch in the usual way but don't take the stitch off the left needle.

2. Pivot the right needle around to the back of the left needle and insert it into the back of the same stitch you just worked. Wrap the yarn around the right needle and pull a loop through the back of the stitch. ▼

3. Slip the worked stitch off the left needle. You now have two new loops on your right needle.

Knit Two Together
k2tog

Insert the right needle knitwise (from front to back) into the next two stitches on the left needle. Knit these two stitches at the same time as if they were one stitch. You have just decreased by one stitch. ▼

Purl Two Together
p2tog

Insert the right needle purlwise (from back to front) into the next two stitches on the left needle. Purl theses two stitches at the same time as if they were one stitch. You have just decreased by one stitch. ▼

Slip, Slip, Knit ssk

This decrease is very similar to a k2tog except that the decrease is knit through the back loops of two stitches at the same time. Working one at a time, slip two stitches to the right needle as if you were going to knit them (knitwise). Insert the tip of the left needle into the front loops of these two stitches. ▼

Now your right needle is in the back loops of the two stitches that are being decreased. Knit these two stitches at the same time through the back loops as if they were one stitch. You have just decreased by one stitch. ▼

Yarn Over yo

Wrap the yarn over the needle creating a loop that will be worked as a new stitch on the next row. The yarnover leaves a distinctive hole in your knitting and is often used decoratively. Yarnovers are worked differently depending on whether you are knitting or purling.

Knit: Bring the yarn forward and lay it over the right needle in a counterclockwise direction ending behind the two needles. Knit the next stitch. Notice that the yarn has made an extra loop on the needle. ▼

Purl: Keeping the yarn in front, wrap it counterclockwise around the right needle. Purl the next stitch. Notice that the yarn has made an extra loop on the needle. ▼

Pick Up and Knit Stitches

Often it is necessary to pick up stitches along a finished edge, such as when you add a button band to a sweater or add a cuff to a slipper. Though the instructions usually say, "Pick up and knit a certain number of stitches," what you really do is pick up the stitches as if you were knitting and leave them on the needle to be worked in the next pass.

1. Working from the right side, insert the right needle from front to back, going under two strands along the edge. ▼

2. Wrap the yarn around the needle as if you were knitting and pull the loop through to the front. Leave the loop (one stitch) on the needle and repeat until you have picked up the number of stitches specified. ▼

Grafting

Grafting, also called Kitchener stitch, weaves together two rows of "live" stitches (not bound off), resulting in an invisible joining.

1. Cut the working yarn, leaving a tail about 18" (46 cm) long. Leave the stitches on the needles; there should be the same number of stitches on each. Hold the needles side by side in the left hand, with the right side facing up. Slide the stitches toward the needle tips.

2. The working yarn will be coming from the first stitch on the back needle. To help explain the steps, we have used a contrasting yarn as the working yarn. Thread the yarn tail on a yarn needle. Draw the yarn through the first stitch on the front needle as if to purl, and leave the stitch on the needle. ▼

3. Keeping the yarn under the needles, draw the yarn through the first stitch on the back needle as if to knit, and leave the stitch on the needle. ▼

4. Draw the yarn through the first stitch on the front needle as if to knit, and slip the stitch off the needle.

5. Draw the yarn through the next stitch on the front needle as if to purl, and leave the stitch on the needle.

6. Draw the yarn through the first stitch on the back needle as if to purl, and slip the stitch off the needle.

7. Draw the yarn through the next stitch on the back needle as if to knit, and leave the stitch on the needle.

8. Repeat steps 4 to 7 until all the stitches have been worked off the needles. ▼

9. If necessary, use the tip of the yarn needle to adjust the tension of the grafting stitches until the join is invisible. With practice, your grafting will need very little adjustment.

10. Draw the yarn to the wrong side and weave in the tail end.

Crochet Techniques

Slip Knot and Chain

All crochet begins with a chain, into which is worked the foundation row for your piece. To make a chain, start with a slip knot. To make a slip knot, make a loop several inches from the end of the yarn, insert the hook through the loop, and catch the tail with the end (1). Draw the yarn through the loop on the hook (2). ▼

After the slip knot, start your chain. Wrap the yarn over the hook (yarn over) and catch it with the hook. Draw the yarn through the loop on the hook. You have now made 1 chain. Repeat the process to make a row of chains. When counting chains, do not count the slip knot at the beginning or the loop that is on the hook (3). ▼

Slip Stitch sl st

The slip stitch is a very short stitch, which is mainly used to join two pieces of crochet together when working in rounds. To make a slip stitch, insert the hook into the specified stitch, wrap the yarn over the hook (1). Then draw the yarn through the stitch and the loop already on the hook (2). ▼

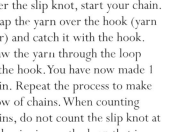

Single Crochet sc

Insert the hook into the specified stitch, wrap the yarn over the hook, and draw the yarn through the stitch so there are two loops on the hook (1). Wrap the yarn over the hook again and draw the yarn through both loops (2). When working in single crochet, always insert the hook through both top loops of the next stitch, unless the directions specify front loop or back loop only.

Single Crochet Two Stitches Together

sc2tog

This decreases the number of stitches in a row or round by one. Insert the hook into the specified stitch, wrap the yarn over the hook, and draw the yarn through the stitch so there are two loops on the hook. Insert the hook through the next stitch, wrap the yarn over the hook, and draw the yarn

through the stitch so there are three loops on the hook (1). Wrap the yarn over the hook again and draw the yarn through all the loops at once (2). ▼

Single Crochet through the Back Loop sc in BL

This creates a distinct ridge on the side facing you. Insert the hook through the back loop only of each stitch, rather than under both loops of the stitch. Complete the single crochet as usual. ▼

Reverse Single Crochet rev sc

This stitch is usually used to create a border. At the end of a row, chain 1 but do not turn. Working backward, insert the hook into the previous stitch (1). Wrap the yarn over the hook, and draw the yarn through the stitch so there are two loops on the hook. Wrap the yarn over the hook again and draw the yarn through both loops. Continue working in the reverse direction (2). ▼

Half Double Crochet hdc

Wrap the yarn over the hook, insert the hook into the specified stitch, and wrap the yarn over the hook again. Draw the yarn through the stitch so there are three loops on the hook (1). Wrap the yarn over the hook and draw it through all three loops at once (2). ▼

Double Crochet dc

Wrap the yarn over the hook, insert the hook into the specified stitch, and wrap the yarn over the hook again. Draw the yarn through the stitch so there are three loops on the hook (1). Wrap the yarn over the hook again and draw it through two of the loops so there are now two loops on the hook (2). Wrap the yarn over the hook again and draw it through the last two loops (3). ▼

Double Crochet Two Stitches Together dc2tog

This decreases the number of stitches in a row or round by one. Wrap the yarn over the hook, insert the hook into the specified stitch, and wrap the yarn over the hook again. Draw the yarn through the stitch so there are three loops on the hook. Wrap the yarn over the hook again and draw it through two of the loops so there are now two loops on the hook. Wrap the yarn over the hook and pick up a loop in the next stitch, so there are now four loops on the hook. Wrap the yarn over the hook and draw through two loops, yarn over and draw through three loops to complete the stitch. ▼

Double Crochet Three Stitches Together dc3tog

This decreases the number of stitches in a row or round by two. Wrap the yarn over the hook, insert the hook into the specified stitch, and wrap the yarn over the hook again. Draw the yarn through the stitch so there are three loops on the hook. Wrap the yarn over the hook again and draw it through two of the loops so there are now two loops on the hook. Wrap the yarn over the hook and pick up a loop in the next stitch, so there are now four loops on the hook.

Wrap the yarn over the hook and draw through two loops. Wrap the yarn over the hook and pick up a loop in the next stitch, so there are now five loops on the hook. Wrap the yarn over the hook and draw through two loops. Wrap the yarn over the hook and draw through the remaining four loops to complete the stitch.

Triple, or Treble Crochet tr

Wrap the yarn over the hook twice, insert the hook into the specified stitch, and wrap the yarn over the hook again. Draw the yarn through the stitch so there are four loops on the hook. Wrap the yarn over the hook again (1) and draw it through two of the loops so there are now three loops on the hook (2).

Wrap the yarn over the hook again and draw it through two of the loops so there are now two loops on the hook (3). Wrap the yarn over the hook again and draw it through the last two loops (4). ▼

Double Triple Crochet dtr

Wrap the yarn over the hook three times, insert the hook into the specified stitch, and wrap the yarn over the hook again. Draw the yarn through the stitch so there are five loops on the hook. Wrap the yarn over the hook again and draw it through two of the loops so there are now four loops on the hook. Wrap the yarn over the hook again and draw it through two of the loops so there are now three loops on the hook. Wrap the yarn over the hook again and draw it through two of the loops so there are now

two loops on the hook. Wrap the yarn over the hook again and draw it through the last two loops. ▼

Front Post Double Crochet FPdc

This stitch usually follows a row of double crochet. Chain 3 to turn. Wrap the yarn over the hook. Working from the front, insert the hook from right to left (left to right for left-handed crocheters) under the post of the first double crochet from the previous row, and pick up a loop (shown). Wrap the yarn over the hook and complete the stitch as a double crochet. ▼

Back Post Double Crochet BPdc

This stitch usually follows a row of double crochet. Chain 3 to turn. Wrap the yarn over the hook. Working from the back, insert the hook from right to left (left to right for left-handed crocheters) under the post of the first double crochet from the previous row, and pick up a loop (shown). Wrap the yarn over the hook and complete the stitch as a double crochet.▼

Front Post Triple Crochet FPtr

Wrap the yarn over the hook twice. Working from the front, insert the hook from right to left (left to right for left-handed crocheters) under the post of the indicated stitch in the row below, and pick up a loop (shown). Wrap the yarn over the hook and complete the triple crochet stitch as usual. ▼

Back Post Triple Crochet BPtr

Wrap the yarn over the hook twice. Working from the back, insert the hook from right to left (left to right for left-handed crocheters) under the post of the indicated stitch in the row below, and pick up a loop. Wrap the yarn over the hook and complete the triple crochet stitch as usual.

Basic Tunisian Stitch

Each row has 2 halves: picking up the loops and working them off.

Make a chain of the desired length.

Row 1 (first half): Keeping all loops on the hook, skip the first chain from the hook (the loop on the hook is the first chain) and draw up a loop in each chain across (1). Do not turn. ▼

Row 1 (second half): Wrap the yarn over the hook and draw it through the first loop. *Wrap the yarn over the hook and draw it through the next 2 loops. Repeat from * across until 1 loop remains. The loop that remains on the hook always counts as the first stitch of the next row (2). ▼

Row 2 (first half): Keeping all loops on the hook, skip the first vertical bar and draw up a loop under the next vertical bar and under each vertical bar across (3). ▼

Row 2 (second half): Work the same as the second half of row 1.

Repeat row 2 for basic Tunisian stitch.

Abbreviations

Knitting Abbreviations

beg	begin	pwise	purlwise
bet	between	rem	remaining or remain
BO	bind off	rep	repeat
CC	contrasting color	rev St stitch	reverse stockinette stitch
cm	centimeter(s)	rib	ribbing
cn	cable needle	rnd(s)	round(s)
CO	cast on	RS	right side
cont	continue	sk	skip
dec	decrease/decreases/decreasing	sl	slip
dpn	double-pointed needle(s)	sl st	slip stitch
g	gram(s)	ssk	slip, slip, knit decrease
inc	increase/increases/increasing	st(s)	stitch(es)
k	knit	St st	stockinette stitch
k2tog	knit two stitches together	tbl	through back loop
k1f&b	knit into front and back loop of same stitch	WS	wrong side
kwise	knitwise	wyb	with yarn in back
m(s)	marker(s)	wyf	with yarn in front
MC	main color	yd.	yard(s)
M1	make one stitch (increase)	yo	yarn over
mm	millimeter(s)	*	repeat from *
oz.	ounce(s)	**	repeat from ** as many times as directed or repeat from a given set of instructions
p	purl	[ ]	repeat instructions in brackets as directed
p1f&b	purl into front and back loop of same stitch	—	number of stitches that should be on the needle or across a row
p2tog	purl two stitches together		
patt	pattern		

Crochet Abbreviations

approx	approximately		mm	millimeter(s)
beg	begin/beginning		oz.	ounce(s)
bet	between		p	picot
BL	back loop(s)		patt	pattern
BP	back post		pc	popcorn
BPdc	back post double crochet		pm	place marker
BPtr	back post triple crochet		prev	previous
CC	contrasting color		rem	remain/remaining
ch	chain		rep	repeat(s)
ch-	refers to chain or space previously made, e.g., ch-1 space		rev sc	reverse single crochet
ch lp	chain loop		rnd(s)	round(s)
ch-sp	chain space		RS	right side(s)
CL	cluster(s)		sc	single crochet
cm	centimeter(s)		sc3tog	single crochet 3 stitches together
cont	continue		sk	skip
dc	double crochet		sl st	slip stitch
dc2tog	double crochet 2 stitches together		sp(s)	space(s)
dc3tog	double crochet 3 stitches together		st(s)	stitch(es)
dec	decrease/decreases/decreasing		tbl	through back loop(s)
dtr	double triple crochet		tch	turning chain
FL	front loop(s)		tog	together
foll	follow/follows/following		tr	triple crochet
FP	front post		tr2tog	triple crochet 2 together
FPdc	front post double crochet		WS	wrong side(s)
FPhdc	front post half-double crochet		yd.	yard(s)
FPtr	front post triple crochet		yo	yarn over
g	gram(s)		*	Repeat from *.
hdc	half double crochet		**	Repeat from ** as many times as directed or repeat from a given set of instructions
inc	increase/increases/increasing		[ ]	Work instructions within brackets as many times as directed
lp(s)	loop(s)		—	At end of row, indicates total number of stitches worked
m	meter(s)			
MC	main color			

Dedication

For my family, who constantly fill my life with joy.

Acknowledgments

Many thanks to the following yarn companies for the generous donation of their yarns for the projects in the book: Aussi Wool, Blue Heron Yarns, DJ International Inc., Knitting Fever, Lily Chin Signature Collection, Lion Brand Yarn, Louet, Noro Yarns, Patons, Plymouth Yarn Company Inc., South West Trading Company, and Tahki Stacy Charles.

Thank you Linda Neubauer, my editor, who is always a pleasure to work with, and who has always been very supportive.

I would also like to thank Paula Alexander and Jeannine Buehler, who helped me knit and crochet some of the items featured in the book.